NIGHTLY SPECIALS

ALSO BY MICHAEL LOMONACO

The '21' Cookbook (with Donna Forsman)

NIGHTLY SPECIALS

125 CONTEMPORARY AMERICAN RECIPES
FOR SPONTANEOUS, CREATIVE COOKING AT HOME

Michael Lomonaco

AND ANDREW FRIEDMAN

PHOTOGRAPHS BY SHIMON AND TAMMAR ROTHSTEIN

WM

WILLIAM MORROW

An Imprint of HarperCollins*Publishers*

HarperCollins books may be purchased for educational, business, or sales promotional use. For information please write: Special Markets Department, HarperCollins Publishers Inc., 10 East 53rd Street, New York, NY 10022.

FIRST EDITION

Designed by Vertigo Design, NYC

Printed on acid-free paper

Library of Congress Cataloging-in-Publication Data

Lomonaco, Michael, 1955–
    Nightly specials: 125 contemporary American recipes for spontaneous, creative cooking at home/Michael Lomonaco and Andrew Friedman.—1st ed.
    p.   cm.
Includes index.
ISBN 0-06-055562-9
1. Cookery.   I. Friedman, Andrew, 1967–   III. Title.

TX714.L.653 2004
641.5—dc22   2004040597

04 05 06 07 08 ❖/TP 10 9 8 7 6 5 4 3 2 1

This book is dedicated to my friends and coworkers at Windows on the World who were senselessly taken from us on September 11, 2001. They will always have a place in my heart and I owe them all a great debt of gratitude for their hard work, friendship, courage, and dignity.

—Michael Lomonaco

CONTENTS

ACKNOWLEDGMENTS

Nobody writes a book, especially a cookbook, by himself. Our heartfelt thanks to the following:

Harriet Bell, our editor at William Morrow, for making Michael's long-time dream a reality;

Shimon and Tammar Rothstein, our brilliant photographers, for their boundless energy, enthusiasm, and talent;

Judith Weber, for her guidance and support;

Jesse Davis, Michael's longtime sous chef, for his diligent recipe testing and invaluable help in the photo shoot;

Pastry chef Daniel Kowal, for testing all the dessert recipes;

Jason Titner, an enthusiastic and dedicated professional cook, for helping to make the photo shoot efficient and fun;

Jean Conlon, Shimon and Tammar's agent, a fair and reasonable voice at all times;

Lucy Baker, of William Morrow, Harriet's able assistant and always a pleasure to work with;

Amy's Bread, Buon Italia, Faicco's Pork Stores, Inc., The Lobster Place, Manhattan Fruit Exchange, Murray's Cheese Shop, Sarabeth's, the Union Square Green Market, Whole Foods Market, and A. Zitto and Sons Bakery, for welcoming us into your places of business and working with us on the market photographs featured in the book;

Sacha Dunn, for sourcing the props used in the food photographs.

—M.L. and A.F.

My thanks to the two chefs who mentored and encouraged me to pursue my dreams: Chef Alain Sailhac, who had so much confidence in me as an apprentice cook and showed me the way, and Chef Daniel Boulud, whose many and abundant talents have been an inspiration to me from the day I met him;

the community of food writers whose ceaseless support has helped shape my career and kept me buoyant through so much these last few years;

the tight-knit and ever supportive family of chefs and restaurateurs who have always made me welcome at their tables for sustenance and succor, and especially to the thousands in the United States and abroad who supported the fundraising efforts of Windows of Hope Family Relief

Fund and, through it, the many family members of my co-workers and colleagues lost on September 11;

Waldy Malouf, Tom Valenti, and Darlene Dwyer, whose vision and determination have made Windows of Hope the great success it is and were there for me in time of great need;

David Emil, Arthur Emil, and Jenny Emil, who owned Windows on the World, who have endlessly encouraged my creativity and been supportive of all of my efforts, both in and out of the kitchen;

Sue Klein, Maureen O'Brien, and Ramiro Jimenez, my longtime colleagues from both Windows and Noche, without whose help and support this book would simply not exist;

Michael Ammirati, a great chef in his own right and an unheralded talent I had the good fortune of working with throughout the time this book was conceived and written. He worked closely with me in developing many of the recipes and ideas in this book. Without him, we would never have had the best the market had to offer every day so that we could cook creatively every night at Windows;

my co-author, Andrew Friedman, for his friendship and great human kindness and for his hard work, vision, and encouragement in making my dream a reality;

my family, especially my brothers Salvatore and Anthony, whose tireless love, support, and guidance has led me so far from our Brooklyn roots;

and especially to Diane, my wife and best friend, without whose love, honesty, and encouragement this book and little else in my life would have happened. Without her by my side life would have little meaning. She is my soul mate and most true companion for life. I love you, Diane, and thank you.

—M.L.

My thanks to the chefs and restaurateurs who have been such great collaborators, teachers, and friends, especially Pino Luongo, Alfred Portale, Bill Telepan, Laurent Tourondel, and Tom Valenti;

my great good pal and collaborator, Michael Lomonaco, who years ago fronted me the cash to buy an engagement ring, and whose focus, determination, talent, and tirelessness are a constant inspiration;

and, most of all, to Caitlin Connelly Friedman, who lovingly nudges me to the next levels of life and career and who makes every day special.

—A.F.

NIGHTLY SPECIALS

SOMETHING

Introduction

SPECIAL, NIGHTLY

F or me, one of the most exciting parts of dining out is when the waiter or waitress gets the attention of the table and announces, "Tonight's specials are . . ."

A lot of diners politely feign interest in what comes next, half listening and waiting to order the dish they've already chosen from the menu. But I perk up and pay close attention, and you should, too; if the chef is creative and devoted to cooking fun and adventuresome food, then the nightly specials are probably sparked by a number of appealing elements.

Nightly specials are where restaurant cooking and home cooking converge. In this book, the same elements that go into a restaurant's nightly specials are used as a springboard for intuitive, improvisational cooking at home. I share the recipes for my favorite nightly specials and provide you with suggestions and tips for making them your own.

Have you ever wondered why restaurants have nightly specials?

There are several reasons, actually, but they all have one thing in common: spontaneity. Nightly specials usually aren't dishes the chef has planned weeks, or even days, in advance. More often than not, he or she dreamed them up that very morning or afternoon. This isn't because the chef is lazy or disorganized. Rather, it's because the market, pantry, and kitchen constantly offer surprises, and the nightly specials are where the chef can take advantage of them.

For example, nightly specials are a way to cook with ingredients whose availability is seasonal or sporadic. When a chef spots spring's first soft-shell crabs at the fish market, he can't wait to get them back to his kitchen; he knows that his customers will be thrilled when they have their first chance of the year to eat soft-shell crabs. He can picture how their eyes will light up when their waiter hits them with that oral addition to the menu. So why wait? He buys enough for the day and rummages through his memory bank and perhaps a written file of past nightly specials to find inspiration. By the time the first dinner guests arrive, he's come up with a simply prepared dish using the crabs to great effect and everybody's happy.

Another reason is that a purveyor, farmer, newspaper or magazine article, or even another chef turns him on to a new and exciting ingredient. For example, a Maine day-boat skipper might introduce him to a regional "hot catch." Eager to see how customers will respond to it, the chef makes the catch the center of a dish that is usually made with salmon. Or a trusted farmer might unveil a new plum he's been nurturing for a year and the chef will devise a version of a Thai beef salad using the fruit in an unusual savory way to see what people think of it.

The third reason is the most practical one: nightly specials are a way to use fresh, uncooked food that remains from the previous few days' marketing. Most restaurants purchase the bulk of their fresh food on a daily basis and, since the refrigerator or shelf life of fresh foods might be just a few days, it is only reasonable to sell today what has been purchased over the past few days. This rotating of inventory can often be a creative trigger; if chicken remains from a slow night, pair it with some shiitake mushrooms and a new special is born. Using all the food we have purchased is not only responsible and economical; it can also be a genuine source of inspiration. Don't think of it as recycling leftovers; consider it a gift, a new way to look at the familiar.

A fourth, equally common, reason is that nightly specials are a way to road-test dishes that might eventually become celebrated regular-menu items without adding them to the printed menu, which is quite a commitment. Fascinated by the spices in Indian cuisine, a chef may decide to cook with them one night because he can no longer resist the temptation. But since his regular guests are accustomed to his Mediterranean food, his new pan-seared breast of chicken with curry vinaigrette is offered as a special so that he can discreetly remove it if it doesn't catch on.

I'm guessing that you can relate to these reasons, because they all apply to you in your home kitchen. There's no set menu in a home, so every dinner is a nightly special. Every meal is fashioned from what the day's market and pantry present. And a good home cook is always looking to learn and improve. Unfortunately, a lot of home cooks get stuck in a rut, turning to the same repertoire over and over, which isn't exciting in the kitchen or at the table.

Today I cook even more frequently at home than I used to, and my pantry is better stocked than ever. It reflects the myriad influences inextricably woven into American cuisine. I don't "cook Italian," or "cook Chinese," or "cook Moroccan." I cook in the American style and American food today happens to have elements of all those cuisines. The way I usually work is by deciding what I am in the mood to eat, or what main ingredient I have on hand or bought because it looked especially good or was on sale at the market, and what cooking method and taste direction I want to take it in. Then I get cooking, without a lot of planning, fuss, or deliberation. The result of that cooking is what I think of as the "nightly special" in my home kitchen.

A number of the dishes in this book are nightly specials that I created over time at Windows on the World, Wild Blue, and '21'; but all are user friendly for home cooks, uncomplicated and easy to follow. This is natural, because a chef teaches these dishes to his line cooks on the same day they will have to cook them for customers. So the specials, almost by definition, have to be easy to cook and plate.

In short, I want to teach you how to create your own nightly specials—simple, loosely improvised dishes that can be selected at the last minute and cooked successfully in relatively little time. But we're not going to reinvent the wheel. Among the dishes you'll find my recipes for a few classics. Classics have endured for a reason and, if they can be spontaneously prepared, there's no reason they can't be special, too. Moreover, classics provide a strong foundation on which to build new dishes, shortening the learning process.

I've tried my best to approach cooking from the perspective of all home cooks, from the food lover who, up until now, has been too intimidated to try cooking at home, to the fearless weekend kitchen warrior who's always ready, willing, and able to try something new.

Whichever of these categories you belong to, or wherever you happen to fall between them, the same overall lessons will benefit you: to use the market to your advantage, to maximize your time, and to cook from your own, unique creative center, so you can make something special every time you set foot in the kitchen.

At first glance, this book probably looks like just another collection of recipes. It is simply organized but its structure and components encourage you to be inventive, use what's on hand, act on impulses you receive from dining out and reading food magazines, and respond to what you see at the market.

Cooking is a unique and accessible form of self-expression. You don't need to follow these recipes slavishly. In fact, I hope they will inspire some new, creative, and ambitious cooking on your part. To that end, a postscript, Your Nightly Specials, appears with every recipe in the book. This is where I'll explain how you can vary the recipe to suit your own taste. This feature enables you to create recipes to suit personal preferences or dietary restrictions and empowers you to roll with the punches at the butcher, fishmonger, or grocer should my ingredient of choice be sold out or simply unavailable.

A NEW

Salads

LEAF

A salad can be the ultimate nightly special for two reasons. First of all, more than almost any other type of dish, a salad takes its cue from the market: salads usually focus on one or two primary ingredients, showcasing them at their height of freshness, with their natural flavor shining through, and not a lot of adornment. In other words, salads are pure.

The second reason is that salad making has evolved into a culinary playground with almost no rules. Where a salad was once guaranteed to comprise leafy greens tossed with vegetables, cheese, and/or poultry, it can today focus on vegetables, meats, or even fish without a green leaf in sight.

I love the salads in this chapter for their versatility. All of them can be first courses, but Cool Roasted Beets with Mint and Mango and Red Onion Salad with Basil Vinaigrette can be side dishes; and Grilled Ginger Chicken Salad and Marinated Salmon Carpaccio with Green Apple and Dill can be small meals on their own.

I also appreciate salads as a way to quickly conjure up the cuisine of different cultures: Artichoke Salad with Pecorino Cheese is a lightning-fast Tuscan starter, Tamarind-Glazed Shrimp Salad is Asian in character, and Curly Endive Salad with Warm Bacon Vinaigrette is an easy take on a French classic.

Versatile, quick, and fresh, that's what a salad is to me—and what the ones in this chapter offer you.

COOL ROASTED BEETS WITH MINT

SERVES 4 TO 6 AS A SALAD OR SMALL MEAL

IF YOU'D NEVER EATEN A FRESH BEET, you'd have a tough time figuring out what to do with a raw one. Rock hard, with a rough, papery skin, beets don't look particularly appetizing, or even edible. But boil or roast one, peel off that wrapper, put a piece in your mouth, and you discover a natural sweetness unlike any other.

Beets require very few supporting ingredients, especially when their natural sweetness is coaxed out by caramelization. Par-cooked beets caramelize more quickly than raw ones, so for this Mediterranean salad, I oven-roast the beets before peeling and quickly sauté them. The roasting concentrates the beet flavor more than boiling the beets.

Ideally, make this salad with small young beets, known sometimes as baby beets. I use these little gems, whether red, yellow, or candy-striped, in salads. They cook quickly and, because their sugars haven't fully developed, the flavor is highly nuanced, allowing you to taste more of the earthy essence of the beet, often masked in mature ones. Look for beets like these in farmers' markets, green markets, or specialty produce stores in the spring and summer; they're worth the hunt. That said, by all means, don't hesitate to use fully grown, fresh red or yellow beets from the supermarket. (You'll see them year-round because they're a good storage crop.) Try to buy them with the beet greens still intact, an indicator of just-picked freshness.

2 pounds red, yellow, or candy-striped beets, ideally small, young, baby beets, scrubbed under cold running water (if the greens are not wilted, chop and add them to the salad greens or save for another use, see page 10; otherwise discard)

2 tablespoons olive oil

3 tablespoons unsalted butter

3 tablespoons chopped mint

1 tablespoon freshly squeezed lemon juice

Fine sea salt and freshly ground black pepper

1 cup mixed torn salad greens

1. Preheat the oven to 375°F.

2. Put the beets in a roasting pan, drizzle with the oil, season with salt and pepper, and toss to coat the beets with the oil. Spread out the beets in a single layer and roast in the oven until tender to a knife tip, 15 to 20 minutes for very small; 45 minutes for very large. Remove the pan from the oven and let the beets cool completely.

3. When they are cool enough to handle, slip the beets out of their skins, using paper towels to grasp them and a paring knife to help loosen the skins. Discard the skins. If using full-grown beets, quarter them or slice into eighths.

4. Melt the butter in a wide, heavy-bottomed sauté pan over medium-high heat. Add the beets and cook, stirring, until lightly caramelized, 4 to 6 minutes. Add the mint and shake and stir the pan to coat the beets. Drizzle the lemon juice over the beets and season with salt and pepper. Transfer the beets to a bowl and let cool to room temperature, approximately 15 minutes. The beets can be made to this point and held at room temperature for up to 1 hour, or covered and refrigerated overnight. Let them come to room temperature before proceeding.

5. Add the salad greens to the bowl and toss.

6. Divide the salad among 4 to 6 salad plates and serve.

Beet greens

Beet greens, a versatile bonus of fresh, young beets, can be eaten raw in a salad, whereas the greens of older beets should be sautéed or braised to soften their bitterness. My favorite way to prepare greens from fully mature beets is to sauté some bacon in a pan until crispy and the fat is rendered. Use a slotted spoon to transfer the bacon to a paper towel–lined plate to drain. Add the greens to the pan and wilt them in the bacon fat over medium heat. Return the bacon to the pan and toss with the greens. Serve this salty, smoky accompaniment alongside braised, roasted, and grilled meat such as Texas-Style Oven-Barbecued Beef Brisket (page 200) and Grilled Pork Chops with Coffee Barbecue Sauce (page 217).

BEETS WITH BASIL, THYME, AND TOASTED, BREADED GOAT CHEESE

ADD ¼ CUP SESAME SEEDS and 2 tablespoons honey along with the mint in step 4.

THE FLAVOR OF FLAT-LEAF PARSLEY, so often treated as mere garnish, really pops when served with an ingredient that offers contrast, like beets. Replace the mint with ¼ cup parsley leaves, but don't chop them.

Sweet beets and tangy, creamy, fresh goat cheese were made for each other. You don't need a specialty cheese source to make this special; just use one of those vacuum-packed goat-cheese logs available in most supermarkets today.

½ cup all-purpose flour

1 cup dried breadcrumbs

1 egg

1 fresh goat-cheese log (12 ounces), cut crosswise into 1-inch discs

2 tablespoons canola oil

2 pounds roasted baby beets

2 tablespoons chopped basil

1 tablespoon chopped thyme

Spread out the flour on a plate and the breadcrumbs on another plate. Beat the egg in a bowl. Dip each piece of cheese into the flour, then the egg, then the breadcrumbs. Pour the oil into a sauté pan and heat it over medium heat until very hot. Fry the cheese discs for 1 minute on each side. Top each salad with one or two cheese discs. Garnish with the basil and thyme.

MANGO AND RED ONION SALAD WITH BASIL VINAIGRETTE

SERVES 4 TO 6 AS A SALAD OR SMALL MEAL

My FAVORITE WAY to come up with a nightly special is to stroll through a market. I scour the aisles not just for what's available but for what's in absolute peak condition, crying out to be prepared and eaten within the next few hours.

Were I to encounter a perfectly ripe mango, my inclination would be not to use it in a dessert, where most people expect to find fruit, but as an appetizer.

Fruit salad has become an unfortunate icon of menus and recipes gone bad; think of all the processed or canned fruit salads you've been served. If you take the time to create your own fruit salad, making thoughtful decisions and enthusiastically celebrating the fruit, you upend convention. That's what we're doing here by combining ripe fruit with savory ingredients like onion, lime juice, and watercress.

I've included a useful technique for dicing a mango, but if you prefer to simply peel, pit, and slice it, that's fine, too.

This refreshing salad is a fine first course and is just as good as a side dish that makes grilled meat and fish come alive. Keep this in mind to serve with Mustard-Glazed Beef Short Ribs (page 203).

2 mangoes, preferably from Florida

½ cup chopped watercress

1 medium red Bermuda onion

1 cup torn mesclun salad greens

Fine sea salt and freshly ground black pepper

3 tablespoons honey, at room temperature

3 tablespoons extra virgin olive oil

3 tablespoons freshly squeezed lime juice

2 tablespoons chopped basil

1 tablespoon soy sauce

¼ teaspoon crushed red pepper flakes, or more to taste

1 tablespoon thinly sliced Fresno chile, or other hot red chile, optional

1. Cut each mango in half, using the tip of your knife to cut around the large pit in the center, then twisting the halves to loosen and remove the pit. With the knife tip, make slashes through the pulp but not the skin. Cut again in the other direction to make crosshatch marks in the fruit. Push the skin of the fruit inside out so that the pulp projects outward. With a spoon, scoop the already-cut pulp into a bowl. Add the watercress to the bowl.

2. Cut the onion in half lengthwise, peel it, and thinly slice from root to stem end in a fine julienne. Add it to the bowl with the mango. Add the greens, season with salt and pepper, and toss gently.

3. Put the honey, oil, lime juice, basil, soy sauce, red pepper flakes, and Fresno pepper, if using, in a small bowl and stir or whisk together. Season with salt, pepper, and more pepper flakes if desired. Pour this vinaigrette over the mango and onion.

4. Divide the salad among 4 salad plates or pass family style from the center of the table as an appetizer or side dish.

YOUR NIGHTLY SPECIALS

SICILIAN-STYLE CITRUS AND ONION SALAD: Red onion plays very well off citrus fruits. There's a classic Sicilian salad of thinly sliced fennel, red onion, and blood oranges that's simply dressed with a sprinkle of salt and a drop of extra virgin olive oil. Follow that by replacing the mangoes with 3 oranges, 4 nectarines, or 2 large grapefruit. Separate the fruit into sections rather than chop it and remove the seeds with a knife tip.

IN THE SUMMER, USE PEACHES, NECTARINES, BLACK PLUMS, OR FIGS. In the late summer, turn to half a honeydew melon, or half a cantaloupe, and—if you like—toss in ½ cup diced Smithfield ham for a salty counterpoint. In the fall or winter, replace the mangoes with 4 ripe, sweet apples or Asian pears. Other tropical fruits work just as well in this recipe. Opt for papaya, sliced star fruit, sliced kiwi fruit, diced pineapple, or a combination, depending on what's available.

FOR A SPICIER SALAD, add 1 or more teaspoons seeded, minced jalapeño to the bowl along with the onion in step 2.

TO MAKE THE SALAD MORE OF A MEAL, add slices of half an avocado to each serving, slicing and fanning them out alongside or underneath the salad; slice up and toss in some cold, leftover Herb-Roasted Capon (page 183) or leftover chicken or duck; top it with grilled chicken breast or grilled shrimp.

CURLY ENDIVE SALAD WITH WARM BACON VINAIGRETTE

SERVES 4 TO 6 AS AN APPETIZER

Sometimes classic dishes can be the most special of all because they evoke associations and memories, not unlike a favorite movie or song. One such dish for me is frisée and lardon salad, which combines feathery, bitter chicory with sautéed bacon. The classic frisée and lardon salad is a true bistro staple that you can find on the menu in innumerable restaurants around the world. This is a supermarket-friendly version that uses curly endive rather than frisée and sliced bacon rather than lardons.

1 cup day-old baguette, cut into ½-inch dice

1 pound sliced bacon, cut crosswise into 1-inch pieces

2 tablespoons chopped shallots

1 tablespoon Dijon mustard

¼ cup white wine vinegar

Fine sea salt and freshly ground black pepper

½ cup olive oil

1 head (about 1½ pounds) curly endive or 2 heads frisée, cut into bite-size pieces, well washed, and dried

1. Preheat the oven to 325°F.

2. Spread out the bread cubes on a cookie sheet and bake until golden, about 7 minutes. Turn the oven off, open the door slightly, and keep the croutons warm in the oven while you make the rest of the salad.

3. Warm a sauté pan over low heat. Put in the bacon and sauté until the fat is rendered and the bacon is crispy, about 8 minutes. Use a slotted spoon to transfer the bacon to a paper towel–lined plate to drain.

4. Pour off and discard all but 2 tablespoons rendered fat from the pan. (Leave more drippings in the pan for a richer dressing.) Add the shallots to the pan over low heat, stir in the mustard and vinegar, and season with salt and pepper. Slowly whisk in the oil to make an emulsified dressing.

5.   Put the endive into a salad bowl. Drizzle the dressing over the greens, add the bacon and croutons, and toss.

6.   Divide the salad among 4 to 6 salad plates and serve while the dressing is still warm and fragrant.

YOUR NIGHTLY SPECIALS

INSTEAD OF BACON, use ½ pound Smithfield ham, cut into small dice, or ½ pound diced smoked turkey, heating them through in ¼ cup warmed olive oil.

FOR THE CROUTONS, slice the baguette into ¼-inch-thick rounds, toast as directed in step 2, and spread with soft, room-temperature goat cheese.

ADD ¼ CUP ROUGHLY CHOPPED TOASTED WALNUTS to the salad, tossing them in while still warm.

ADD A TABLESPOON OR TWO OF CRUMBLED ROQUEFORT or other blue cheese. Be sure the cheese is at room temperature.

MAKE A MEAL OF THIS, either by doubling the recipe or by topping each salad with a poached egg.

ROASTED SUMMER GARDEN VEGETABLES WITH BLUE CHEESE

SERVES 4 TO 6 AS AN APPETIZER

I GREW UP WITH a small but plentiful backyard garden tended by my father, Frank. Like many families with a garden we often reached a point where what to do with all the vegetables became an issue. If you know that feeling, or get carried away when you visit a farmers' market or roadside stand, try this salad as a main course, or make a different version for a few days in a row, varying the vegetables.

The best blue-veined cheeses are made in small batches and have a rich and creamy taste and sharp quality without being too salty, gritty, or soapy. I appreciate blue cheese for its affinity with other ingredients such as beets, black pepper, cucumbers, tomatoes, and various herbs. One of my favorite ways to use American-made blue cheese is in a salad like this one, a modern answer to the old iceberg lettuce with blue cheese dressing.

Because our cravings don't always adhere to the calendar, I've created this all-season recipe, which roasts the tomatoes so you're not restricted to the late summer. Serve this with your favorite bread to soak up the delicious vegetable juices.

8 ounces blue cheese

Fine sea salt

2 cups green beans snapped in half

1 medium green zucchini, sliced crosswise into ½-inch rounds

1 medium yellow squash, sliced crosswise into ½-inch rounds

1 small eggplant (about 1 pound), sliced crosswise into ½-inch rounds

2 red bell peppers, stemmed and seeded, sliced lengthwise into crescent shapes

6 garlic cloves

⅔ cup olive oil

Freshly ground black pepper

3 to 4 plum tomatoes (about 1 pound total), sliced lengthwise into crescent shapes

⅓ cup balsamic vinegar

3 tablespoons chopped thyme

1 head Boston lettuce, cored, leaves separated, washed, and dried

Extra virgin olive oil

GRILLED SUMMER GARDEN
VEGETABLES WITH BLUE
CHEESE: While oven-roasting in
the summer seems counterintu-
itive, it is simpler than grilling,
which asks you to tend to each
vegetable individually. But if you
happen to love grilling, you can
certainly grill the vegetables. Just
coat them with oil and grill over
an open fire, in a vegetable basket,
or on a fine-mesh grate designed
for this purpose. Drizzle the
grilled vegetables with the thyme
and balsamic vinegar, serve them
in the Boston lettuce basket, and
drizzle with extra virgin olive oil.

BRUSCHETTA: When the roasted
garlic cloves are cool enough to
handle, make a small slit in each
one and squeeze the garlic into a
bowl. Mash it and spread on
grilled French bread to make a
bruschetta to accompany this
salad or other dishes. (The garlic
puree can be covered and refrigerated for up to 3 days.)

SUBSTITUTE FOR THE BLUE
CHEESE an aged, sharp cheddar or
Spanish sheep's-milk cheese like
Manchego.

1. Preheat the oven to 450°F. Remove the blue cheese from the refrigerator, cut it into 4 to 6 equal pieces (1 per serving), and set aside to soften
at room temperature while you prepare the salad.

2. Fill a large, heavy-bottomed pot halfway with water and bring it to a
boil over high heat. Fill a large bowl halfway with ice water. Salt the boiling
water and add the green beans. Blanch for 2 minutes, then drain the beans
and transfer to the ice water to stop the cooking. Drain again and set aside.

3. Put the zucchini, squash, eggplant, peppers, and garlic in a roasting
pan. Drizzle with half the olive oil, season with salt and pepper, and gently
toss. Spread them out as evenly as possible. Roast until the vegetables
begin to brown, 20 minutes, shaking the pan from time to time to keep
them from scorching or sticking.

4. Meanwhile, put the tomatoes and beans in a bowl and drizzle with the
remaining olive oil. Season with salt and pepper and toss gently by hand.
Add the tomatoes and beans to the pan with the roasting vegetables and
let roast for another 10 minutes. Drizzle the vinegar over the vegetables
and roast until the tomatoes begin to char, another 10 minutes.

5. Remove the pan from the oven and sprinkle the thyme over the vegetables. Stir gently to combine. Taste, adjust the seasoning if necessary, and
let cool slightly. Use a pair of tongs to fish out and discard the garlic cloves,
or use them to make croutons (see Your Nightly Specials).

6. Make a bed of lettuce leaves on each of 4 to 6 salad plates, nesting
them together to form a container for the vegetables. Spoon equal quantities of vegetables into each lettuce nest, being sure to include a good mix
of vegetables in each serving.

7. Crumble 1 portion of cheese over each serving, drizzle with extra virgin olive oil, and serve warm.

ARTICHOKE SALAD WITH PECORINO CHEESE

SERVES 4 TO 6 AS AN APPETIZER

IN TUSCANY, when spring vegetables are just beginning to emerge, many of them are consumed raw: shelled fava beans are drizzled with olive oil and topped with shavings of young pecorino Toscano cheese; green peas are tossed straight from the pod into salads; and young artichokes are shaved paper thin on a mandoline, then simply dressed with olive oil, lemon juice, and grated cheese.

This recipe epitomizes market-driven cooking, because, quite simply, you will either find suitable artichokes in the market or you won't. Choose only the smallest, tenderest of the fresh artichokes, which actually have two seasons, one in spring and one in the early fall; once they have developed a purple choke inside, they are no longer appropriate for raw salads. Serve this before Fettuccine with Mushrooms and Asparagus (page 87) or Sicilian Shrimp and Couscous (page 130).

1 pound tiny artichokes, trimmed (see page 22), stems, if any, left attached and carefully peeled

¼ cup extra virgin olive oil

3 tablespoons freshly squeezed lemon juice

2 cups torn mesclun salad greens

¼ cup loosely packed basil

¼ cup chopped flat-leaf parsley

12 to 18 shards (3 per serving) pecorino Romano cut lengthwise with a vegetable peeler

A few grinds black pepper

1. Peel away the first layers of outer leaves from each artichoke, the darkest coarse ones, until you reach the pale, green-yellow leaves.

2. Slice the artichokes paper thin lengthwise on a mandoline, collecting the slices in a bowl. Immediately pour 2 tablespoons of the oil and 1 tablespoon of the lemon juice into the bowl and toss to combine well. Let the artichokes marinate for 10 minutes, but no longer, or they may blacken from oxidation.

3. Pour the remaining 1 tablespoon lemon juice and 2 tablespoons oil into a separate bowl and whisk together. Add the salad greens, basil, and parsley to the bowl and toss well.

4. Mound some of the dressed greens in the center of each of 4 to 6 cold or chilled plates. Top each plate with some of the artichoke slices and 3 shards of cheese. Finish with a few grinds of black pepper and serve.

Buying and trimming artichokes

Artichokes range from golfball size to large as grapefruits. They are all fully mature; the large ones come from the top of the plant, the smaller from the bottom. (If buying larger artichokes, seek out those that are unblemished and free of black spots, with tight, closed tops.) When you squeeze them, they should squeak with moisture. If not using them immediately, refresh them with a gentle spray of cold water, put them in a plastic bag, and refrigerate overnight. Before using the artichokes, wash them carefully in lukewarm water. Before steaming larger ones, trim the pointy ends of the leaves (cut off the top ¼ inch) and tear off and discard the darkest outer leaves and any blemished outer leaves.

YOUR NIGHTLY SPECIALS

SUBSTITUTES FOR SMALL ARTICHOKES: Steam larger artichokes. Put trimmed artichokes in a large, heavy-bottomed pot, stem end down, and pour in enough water to rise halfway up the artichoke(s). Squeeze lemon juice (1 lemon for every 4 artichokes) into the water, cover, bring to a boil over high heat, then lower the heat and let simmer until a leaf pulls free with a gentle tug, 25 to 35 minutes.

Drain the artichokes, cool and peel, and use the hearts to make this salad.

1 pound very young pencil asparagus, shaved with a peeler from end to end, eaten raw or—if you like—blanched, shocked in ice water, and drained.

1 pound fresh, young green zucchini, shaved thinly crosswise with a mandoline or very sharp knife.

SUBSTITUTE SALTY PARMIGIANO-REGGIANO or California dry Jack cheese for the pecorino Romano.

Thinly slice pecorino Romano or Parmigiano-Reggiano using a vegetable peeler or an old-fashioned cheese slicer with a wide blade and slot. Layer over the salad.

If you can't find peas and favas tender enough to eat raw, expand the salad by adding to the asparagus a total of ½ cup fresh peas and/or shelled favas, blanching them, shocking them in cold water, and draining them before using.

High-quality extra virgin olive oil and/or balsamic vinegar drizzled over each serving would be a smart finishing touch.

GRILLED GINGER CHICKEN SALAD

SERVES 4

There are only a few tablespoons of grated ginger in this main-course salad, but what peppery zing they impart! Ginger offers a great opportunity to let the market speak to you; you might decide to make this dish by spotting a basket of superior ginger and thinking, "That's what I want to celebrate tonight." Or you might have ginger left over from another recipe and be looking for a way to use it today.

When shopping for fresh ginger, find a piece that looks and feels firm to the touch with no spots or blemishes. On the West Coast, you might be lucky enough to encounter young, pink ginger—probably grown in Hawaii—which has almost no fiber; don't pass up the chance to use it in this recipe. You could make this at any time of year, using a grill pan or broiler in the colder months, but it's really meant for summer, when you can grill the chicken outdoors and enjoy the surprisingly cooling effect of the ginger.

2 tablespoons peeled, grated ginger (see page 24)

¼ cup soy sauce

¼ cup rice wine

⅓ cup vegetable oil

2 tablespoons freshly squeezed lime juice

1 jalapeño pepper, seeded and minced

¼ cup coarsely chopped cilantro

2 pounds boneless chicken breasts, skin intact

1½ cups assorted small tomatoes such as small heirloom, cherry, or grape, halved or quartered if necessary to a uniform size

8 large radishes, thinly sliced

1 pink grapefruit, segmented

1 medium avocado, thinly sliced lengthwise (see page 24)

2 scallions, thinly sliced crosswise

1. Stir together the ginger, soy sauce, rice wine, oil, lime juice, chile, and cilantro in a bowl. Pour half the marinade into a container, cover, and refrigerate. (This will be the dressing for the salad.)

FOR THE CHICKEN, SUBSTI-
TUTE an equal quantity of
roasted, cubed duck breast or
grilled, sliced pork tenderloin. Use
the same marinade for both.
Roast the duck according to the
instructions on page 193. Grill the
tenderloin, turning several times,
for 7 to 8 minutes total cooking
time, or until it has only the
faintest trace of pink at its center.

THE SALAD, WITHOUT THE
CHICKEN OR AVOCADO, is a
perfect accompaniment to Grilled
Shrimp Kabobs with Corn Salsa
(page 139) or Black Currant–
Lacquered Duck Breast (page 193).

2. Put the chicken breasts in a shallow baking dish or other vessel. Pour the remaining marinade over the chicken, cover with plastic wrap, and let marinate, refrigerated, for 6 hours, or overnight.

3. Preheat a grill or grill pan.

4. Gently stir the tomatoes, radishes, and grapefruit together in a bowl. Set aside.

5. Remove the chicken from the baking dish and discard the marinade. Grill the chicken breasts until the juices run clear when pierced with the tip of a knife or fork, 5 to 6 minutes per side. Set the chicken aside to cool. When cool enough to handle, cut the chicken into 1-inch cubes. Add the chicken to the tomato salad and drizzle the dressing over the salad. (To prevent contaminating the food, do not under any circumstances use the marinade that dressed the raw chicken.) Toss gently.

6. To serve, arrange a few slices of avocado in the center of each of 4 plates. Spoon some salad over each avocado base and scatter some scallions over each serving.

Ginger

Choose the freshest ginger available, recognizable by unblemished skin that is smooth and not torn. Ginger's cut end will show its age; if it appears fibrous, the ginger has been sitting around too long. To peel ginger, use a teaspoon to scrape the papery skin off; a vegetable peeler removes too much of the ginger itself.

Avocado

Cut the avocado in half from top to bottom, running a large knife around the pit. As if you are striking with an ax, drive the heel of the knife (the sharp end of the knife nearest the handle) into the pit, wiggle the knife to loosen the pit, and pull the pit out. Use a large spoon to scoop out the avocado in one piece.

CHARRED BEEF AND CRISP VEGETABLES

SERVES 4

IF YOU'RE INTRIGUED BY THE REFRESHING, herbaceous heat of Thai food, this is an easy way to try your hand at making it in your own kitchen. Don't worry about the number of ingredients, because many of them, such as rice wine and peanut oil, have become standard members of the Western pantry. And Thai fish sauce, if you don't have it already, is available in many supermarkets, so this salad can be shopped in a matter of minutes, just as long as it takes to procure the produce and flank steak. Pair this with Coconut-Scented Basmati Rice (page 97) or Quinoa "Risotto" with Toasted Hazelnuts and Dried Currants (page 106).

2 celery stalks, cut into small dice

1 small seedless cucumber, cut into small dice

2 carrots, peeled and cut into julienne

1 pound fresh, raw baby spinach leaves, well washed in several changes of cold water, and dried

1 pint cherry tomatoes, halved

¼ cup rice wine vinegar

½ cup rice wine

¼ cup vegetable oil

3 tablespoons peanut oil

1 pound beef flank steak, sliced against the grain into ¼-inch-thick strips

Fine sea salt and freshly ground black pepper

2 tablespoons peeled, grated ginger

2 teaspoons ground cumin seed

6 to 8 basil leaves, finely shredded by hand

3 tablespoons Thai fish sauce (nam pla; see following page)

2 tablespoons cornstarch dissolved in 2 tablespoons warm water

1. Put the celery, cucumber, carrots, spinach, and tomatoes in a bowl.

2. Put the rice wine vinegar and rice wine in another bowl and whisk together, then whisk in the vegetable oil. Drizzle this dressing over the vegetables, toss, and let marinate while you prepare and cook the beef.

3. You may need to do the following in batches: Heat some or all of the peanut oil in a wok or wide, heavy-bottomed sauté pan until very hot. Add the beef, season with salt and pepper, and cook quickly, stirring constantly,

SUBSTITUTE FOR THE BEEF
small, peeled shrimp, sautéed
until firm and pink, about 3 minutes; chicken breast, cut into
½-inch-thick strips, sautéed until
firm and no pink remains, 6 to 7
minutes; or pork tenderloin, cut
into ½-inch-thick strips and
sautéed until well browned,
about 7 minutes.

SUBSTITUTE 1 CUP BROCCOLI
FLORETS or 1 cup diced zucchini
for the carrots.

ADD ½ CUP MUNG BEAN
SPROUTS or daikon radish to
the vegetables in step 1 for
more crunch.

over high heat. As soon as the beef is well seared and before it overcooks,
2 to 3 minutes, remove it from the pan and set it aside on a plate. If working in batches, immediately repeat this process with the remaining peanut
oil and beef. When the second batch is similarly cooked, return the first
batch to the pan just to reheat it.

4. Add the ginger, cumin, basil, fish sauce, and dissolved cornstarch to the
pan. Cook, stirring, until the mixture thickens and coats the beef, 1 to 2
minutes.

5. To serve, divide the vegetables among individual plates and top with
some of the hot beef; the heat should just wilt the vegetables.

Thai fish sauce

Thai fish sauce, or *nam pla,* is part of a long line of seasoning sauces that
extends all the way back to the Roman Empire, where fermented fish
paste was a kitchen staple. The fish sauce alone is a great seasoning
agent, akin to anchovies in Western cooking. Its use has popped up in
many cultures, including Vietnamese and Cambodian.

TAMARIND-GLAZED SHRIMP SALAD

SERVES 6 AS AN APPETIZER OR 4 AS A MAIN COURSE

As a lifelong New Yorker, I've been privileged to enjoy foods and cooking styles from around the world, right in my own concrete backyard. In ethnic neighborhoods all over Brooklyn, Queens, and the Bronx, small cafés and restaurants feature dishes I am grateful to have been able to sample so close to home. They have influenced my palate, my cooking, and my kitchen style. One ingredient I've learned to love is tamarind, a thick, sour fruit paste with an acidic, apricot-date flavor. Tamarind appears in dishes from places as diverse as China, India, the Caribbean, and Latin America. The combination of tamarind and sweet honey is the epitome of what sweet and sour should be. Serve this as a starter before Sea Bass Steamed with Lemongrass and Chili-Coconut Broth (page 155).

2 tablespoons tamarind paste

2 tablespoons sugar

½ cup rice wine

¼ cup honey, at room temperature

2 tablespoons Thai fish sauce (nam pla; see page 27)

½ pound seedless cucumber, scored with a channeling knife or fork and cut crosswise into thin slices with a vegetable peeler

1 pint cherry tomatoes, quartered

1 cup pea shoots, mung beans, or other sprouts

2 tablespoons peanut oil

3 to 4 whole Thai chiles or 1 tablespoon seeded, minced jalapeño pepper

2 tablespoons peeled, grated ginger

1 pound jumbo shrimp, peeled and deveined

¼ cup shelled, unsalted peanuts, crushed or coarsely ground

1. Pour 2 tablespoons hot water over the tamarind and sugar in a small bowl. Stir until the mixture comes together in a paste. Add the rice wine, honey, and fish sauce and stir well to combine. Set aside.

2. Arrange the cucumber slices in an overlapping pattern around the edge of a serving platter. Arrange the tomatoes decoratively around the

NIGHTLY SPECIALS

YOUR

AN EQUAL WEIGHT OF SEA SCALLOPS, thinly sliced monkfish fillets, or diced boneless chicken meat would be a good alternative to the shrimp. If using chicken, increase the cooking time to about 7 minutes.

platter, overlapping the cucumbers where necessary. Arrange the pea shoots in a heap in the center of the platter. Set the platter aside.

3. Heat the peanut oil in a large wok or sauté pan over high heat. Add the chiles and heat through for 30 seconds. Add the ginger, cook for 30 seconds, then add the shrimp and stir-fry for 2 to 3 minutes. Add the tamarind glaze and bring to a boil. Toss or stir the shrimp well to coat in the glaze. Cook just until the shrimp turn firm and pink, 1 to 2 minutes more. If using whole Thai chiles, remove them with tongs and discard.

4. Spoon the shrimp over the pea shoots, scatter the peanuts over the top, and serve the salad family style from the center of the table.

MARINATED SALMON CARPACCIO WITH GREEN APPLE AND DILL

SERVES 4 AS AN APPETIZER

First served at Harry's Bar in Venice, a carpaccio is traditionally made with raw beef. Modern chefs, beginning with Gilbert Le Coze at Le Bernardin in New York City, reinvented the carpaccio as a vehicle for everything from sea bass to lamb. His seafood carpaccio took raw fish out of the sushi realm. The first fish carpaccio I ever prepared was, appropriately enough, a nightly special: I was a young cook at Le Cirque and Chef Alain Sailhac put it on the menu one day and gave me the honor of preparing it.

Buy and use fish only from a trusted fish market when preparing this, or any, dish in which raw fish will be consumed.

1 pound super fresh (sushi-grade) salmon fillet, in 1 boneless piece

1 lime, zest grated with a microplane or fine-holed grater, pith discarded, fruit segmented, pithy pulp reserved

1 small orange, zest grated with a microplane or fine-holed grater, pith discarded, fruit segmented, pithy pulp reserved

1 teaspoon Dijon mustard

½ teaspoon fennel seeds, ground in a spice grinder

1 shallot, cut into small dice

3 tablespoons olive oil

1 large green apple

3 tablespoons coarsely chopped dill

1. Lay out the salmon on an immaculately clean work surface. With a very sharp, thin-bladed knife, ideally a boning or salmon knife, horizontally slice the salmon as thinly as possible, working on a slight bias from top to bottom. You should have about 12 slices (3 per portion).

2. Lay about 3 salmon slices on each of 4 chilled or cold salad plates, pressing them together to form a single layer covering the surface of the plate.

NIGHTLY SPECIALS

FOR THE APPLE, SUBSTITUTE
Asian pear or, for a take off on
prosciutto and melon, cubes of
cantaloupe or honeydew.

REPLACE THE SALMON with
sushi-grade tuna and the apple
with 1 small mango and 1 small
papaya.

SERVE THE SALMON AS A
CEVICHE: Omit the apple. Slice
the salmon into thin strips and
put it in a bowl with the other
ingredients. Toss and let marinate
for 10 minutes, then serve in
chilled martini glasses or on
chilled salad plates.

3. Squeeze the lime and orange pulp into a small bowl, extracting as
much juice as possible. Add the mustard, fennel seeds, shallot, and olive oil
and whisk to combine. Add the lime and orange segments. Spoon a scant
layer of this marinade evenly over each portion of salmon and marinate in
the refrigerator for 10 minutes while you prepare the apple.

4. Peel the apple and use a vegetable peeler to cut it into a fine julienne.
Put it in a small bowl and add the lime and orange zests and dill. Toss and
set aside.

5. Mound some dressed apple in the center of each carpaccio and serve
at once.

DAILY
Snacks, Sandwiches, and Pizzas
BREADS

Most people take the foods in this chapter for granted. Pizzas, sandwiches, and snacks are what you take out when you don't feel like cooking, or grab on the run when you don't have time to settle down for a meal. I believe that reinventing or revisiting food that we hardly notice anymore can be potent inspiration for nightly specials and welcome revelations for the people you're cooking for.

There isn't much finger food in this chapter, but its message couldn't be more important: everything that you cook for others should be special. It doesn't have to be big and complicated, but it should be thoughtfully selected and prepared. The finger food in this chapter will show you how to make a suitable first impression without pulling a kitchen all-nighter.

As for sandwiches, well, they are one of the easiest ways to be impromptu and creative, and to use the food in your pantry in tandem with whatever is market fresh. Here, too, we're going to go beyond the standard combinations of meat, cheese, and dressings usually found between two slices of bread. We're only exposing the tip of this iceberg; keep going on your own and explore open-faced sandwiches, avail yourself of great, local, hearth-baked bread, and take classic sandwiches in new directions, or simply upgrade them by paying a little extra attention to the quality of the ingredients. For example, a Philadelphia cheese steak with prime aged beef and imported or artisan cheeses turns a regional fast-food treat into something unique.

Then there's pizza, another all-too-commonplace food that we love but take for granted, and in some ways lack respect for. Rare are the locations in the country where you can't line up a pizza with a quick call to the local shop or branch of some national chain. So why make your own? Because you'll have an endless choice of toppings, be able to control the amounts of sauce and cheese, your homemade pizza will taste better, and, perhaps best of all, the cheese will never get stuck to the top of the box. And how's this for another reason: pizza itself can be an excuse for a party where you top and bake a variety of pizzas throughout the evening, serving them with specially chosen microbrew beers and excellent wines.

A few pizza-making suggestions: use a pizza stone or bread stone, available for about twenty dollars; they make a big difference in the crust because they contain and transfer the heat to the dough by direct contact. (If making pizzas or flatbreads in a baking sheet, like deep-dish Chicago-style pizza, you don't need a stone; a well-seasoned cookie sheet will do.) I recommend that you also invest in a pizza peel, one of those large, wooden spatulas that help slide the pizza in and out of the oven gracefully. It's very helpful and will make you feel like a pro the first time you use it.

Don't think of new variations as pizzas. Instead, think of them, and cook them, like flatbread. Use the same dough, but instead of making a perfect circle with a rolled edge, fashion a rustic shape with no defined edge. This gives you license to top it with anything you like, perhaps even leaving out cheese and tomato altogether. It works for me: in this chapter, I present the classic pizzas as "pizzas" and more personal ones as "flatbread."

LEEK AND ONION TARTLETS WITH AMERICAN CAVIAR

MAKES ABOUT 12 TARTLETS, ENOUGH TO SERVE 4 AS AN HORS D'OEUVRE

IF THERE'S ONE INGREDIENT that says "special," it's caviar. For generations, nothing has compared to the celebratory connotations of the tiny eggs of Caspian sturgeon. But did you know that there are also many fine alternatives produced here in the United States? They're far less expensive than their Russian and Iranian counterparts and, while they may not have the same mystique, they offer comparable flavor and texture. The best of them come from domestic salmon, paddlefish, and whitefish.

This crisp finger food lets the caviar do most of the work. You fashion simple pastry cups by molding phyllo dough to the wells of a mini-muffin tin. You can use these pastry cups as a vehicle for other ingredients or combinations.

6 sheets phyllo dough, thawed according to package directions

4 tablespoons (½ stick) unsalted butter, melted

1 white onion, cut into small dice (about ½ cup)

1 red onion, cut into small dice (about ½ cup)

1 small leek (white and light green parts), split, washed, and cut into 1½-inch-long julienne (about 1 cup)

1 cup crème fraîche or sour cream

2 ounces American sturgeon black caviar or salmon roe

2 tablespoons chopped chives

1. Preheat the oven to 375°F.

2. Lightly brush each sheet of phyllo with 2 tablespoons melted butter, stacking the sheets to form 2 three-layered stacks. Use a biscuit cutter, glass, or ring mold to cut each stack into rounds roughly twice as large as the wells of a mini-muffin tin. Brush some of the melted butter into the wells and put 1 round into each well to form a pastry cup by gently pressing it down. Bake the pastry cups until they are golden brown and crisp, about 8 minutes.

TRY THESE FILLINGS IN THE PHYLLO TARTS:

- minced ham and melted Swiss or Gruyère cheese
- smoked trout, crumbled and mixed with mayonnaise and capers
- minced tomato and basil drizzled with olive oil
- very small shrimp, poached, cooled, and dressed with mayonnaise and tarragon

TO SERVE THE TARTLETS AS A FIRST COURSE, double the quantities in the ingredient list. Cut the phyllo stacks into larger circles and shape them to 3-inch ring molds. Bake as directed and fill each pastry shell with double the quantity of onion-leek mixture, sour cream, and caviar.

3. Meanwhile, pour 2 tablespoons melted butter into a wide, heavy-bottomed sauté pan and set it over medium heat. Add the white and red onions and leek and sauté until wilted but not browned, about 4 minutes. Remove the pan from the heat and allow the vegetables to cool to room temperature.

4. When the phyllo has baked and the vegetables have cooled, arrange the tartlet shells on a serving platter. Assemble the tartlets by spooning a portion of the leek-onion mixture into the bottom of each pastry cup. Add about 1 tablespoon crème fraîche to each cup and top with a scant teaspoon each of caviar and chives. Serve.

CORN CAKES WITH SMOKED SALMON

SERVES 4 TO 6 AS AN HORS D'OEUVRE OR APPETIZER

THIS IS A VALUABLE RECIPE to have in your repertoire because it can be used in a number of ways. The combination of small corn cakes and salmon is a sophisticated passed hors d'oeuvre; plated alongside a salad, it makes a first course or light lunch that could precede poultry, meat, or even cooked fish; and, because it features smoked fish, a brunch staple, it's just as much at home at a weekend breakfast as at the dinner table.

1 cup cornmeal

½ cup all-purpose flour

2 teaspoons baking soda

Fine sea salt

2 eggs

1 cup milk

2 tablespoons unsalted butter, melted, at room temperature

About ¼ cup vegetable oil

1 cup sour cream

¼ cup chopped chives, plus a few whole chives for garnish

4 ounces smoked salmon, thinly sliced horizontally, then into thin strips

1. Stir the cornmeal, flour, baking soda, and 1 teaspoon salt together in a bowl. Whisk the eggs in another bowl, then whisk the eggs, milk, and butter into the dry ingredients to make a batter. Cover with plastic wrap and refrigerate for 30 minutes.

2. Pour a thin layer of vegetable oil into a large sauté pan and heat it over medium heat until a drop of batter sizzles on contact. Begin to spoon batter, 2 to 3 tablespoons at a time, into the pan to make pancake-like corn cakes, cooking them until lightly crisped and golden on both sides, about 2 minutes per side. Cook in batches, cleaning the pan if it becomes messy and adding additional oil as necessary. Keep the cakes warm by covering with foil while you finish cooking the remaining batter.

3. In a small bowl, stir together the sour cream and chopped chives.

4. Arrange the corn cakes on a serving dish or platter, top each with a dollop of the cream, and finish with some of the sliced salmon. Garnish with whole chives and serve.

YOUR NIGHTLY SPECIALS

INSTEAD OF SALMON, use smoked trout, smoked sturgeon, or smoked mackerel. Gravlax (salmon cured with sugar, salt, and herbs) would also be a fine alternative.

THE CORN CAKES ALONE ARE A GOOD ACCOMPANIMENT to the Marinated Salmon Carpaccio with Green Apple and Dill (page 31).

TOP THE CORN CAKES and smoked salmon with salmon roe or sturgeon caviar.

BRUSCHETTA

A BRUSCHETTA, or crostino, is an Italian hors d'oeuvre that features a slice of country bread, usually toasted or grilled, topped with any number of things. The two best known toppings are diced tomato and basil and sautéed chopped chicken livers. But the format offers a virtually unlimited number of possibilities; a bruschetta can be topped with beans, cheese, vegetables, and meat. When grilled, it can be a resourceful way to use day-old bread.

Here are three of my favorite versions. Let the seasons dictate which one you make: the tomato bruschetta is a vehicle for late-summer tomatoes at the height of flavor; the chicken liver's rustic quality is best suited to the fall and winter; and the white bean calls on dried beans, a pantry staple, so it can be enjoyed at any time.

CHICKEN LIVER BRUSCHETTA
SERVES 4

1 Italian loaf or baguette, cut crosswise into thin rounds

¼ cup olive oil

1 pound chicken livers, rinsed and thoroughly cleaned

Fine sea salt and freshly ground black pepper

¼ cup minced shallots

½ cup sherry vinegar

1 tablespoon minced flat-leaf parsley

1 tablespoon minced thyme

1. Preheat the oven to 350°F. Put the bread rounds on a cookie sheet, brush them with 2 tablespoons of the oil, and toast in the oven until golden and crispy, about 10 minutes. Remove the sheet from the oven and set aside.

2. Heat the remaining 2 tablespoons oil in a heavy-bottomed sauté pan over medium heat. Add the chicken livers, season with salt and pepper, and

cook until browned on one side, approximately 2 minutes. Turn the livers over and add the shallots. Cook, shaking the pan to prevent scorching, until the livers are fully cooked, about 4 more minutes. Pour in the vinegar and stir, cooking until it evaporates, about 5 minutes. Remove the pan from the heat and transfer its contents to a bowl. Stir in the parsley and thyme.

3. When cool, mash the chicken liver mixture with the back of a wooden spoon until almost spreadable.

4. Serve the toasted bread from a platter with the chicken livers alongside in a bowl, and a spoon or knife for spreading them on the bread.

GARDEN-FRESH TOMATO BRUSCHETTA
SERVES 4

1 Italian loaf or baguette, cut crosswise into thin rounds

2 tablespoons olive oil

6 super ripe (soft) plum tomatoes, cut into small dice

10 basil leaves, torn into small pieces

1 garlic clove, minced

¼ cup extra virgin olive oil

1 tablespoon balsamic vinegar

Fine sea salt and freshly ground black pepper

1. Preheat the oven to 350°F. Put the bread rounds on a cookie sheet, brush them with the olive oil, and toast in the oven until golden and crispy, about 10 minutes. Remove the sheet from the oven and set aside.

2. Put the tomatoes, basil, garlic, extra virgin olive oil, and vinegar in a bowl. Season with salt and pepper and stir gently to combine.

3. Arrange the toasted bread on a platter and top each slice with a spoonful of the tomato mixture so the bread can soak up the flavorful juice. Serve at once.

YOU CAN TOP THE TOASTED BREAD WITH ALMOST ANYTHING. Some of my personal favorites are:

- olive spread (tapenade)
- creamy fresh goat cheese, softened at room temperature, with herbs or cracked black pepper stirred in
- cold leftover steak or filet mignon in thin slices, topped with Basil Pesto (page 93)
- cold leftover chicken, in small dice, with herb or pesto mayonnaise

1 cup dried cannellini beans

1 medium onion, cut into small dice

2 thyme sprigs plus 1 tablespoon chopped thyme leaves

1 bay leaf

Fine sea salt and freshly ground black pepper

1 Italian loaf or baguette, cut crosswise into thin rounds

2 tablespoons olive oil

½ cup extra virgin olive oil, plus more for serving

2 garlic cloves, minced

1. Soak the beans overnight, or put the beans in a pot, cover with water, and bring to a boil over high heat. Remove from the heat and set aside, covered, for 1 hour.

2. Drain the beans and transfer them to a heavy-bottomed pot. Add the onion, thyme sprigs, bay leaf, and 4 cups water. Bring to a boil over high heat, then lower the heat and let simmer, covered, for 45 minutes. Stir in 1 teaspoon salt and 1 teaspoon pepper, cover, and continue to simmer until the beans are tender, about 45 minutes more.

3. Meanwhile, preheat the oven to 350°F. Put the bread slices on a cookie sheet, brush them with the olive oil, and toast in the oven until golden and crispy, about 10 minutes. Remove the sheet from the oven and set aside.

4. Drain the beans. Use tongs to discard the thyme sprigs and bay leaf.

5. Warm the extra virgin olive oil in a heavy-bottomed pot over low heat. Add the garlic and beans, taste and adjust the seasoning with salt and pepper, and cook, stirring, for 4 minutes.

6. Remove the pot from the heat and puree the mixture in a food processor fitted with a steel blade until smooth and creamy. Stir in the thyme leaves.

7. Transfer the mixture to a bowl and drizzle with extra virgin olive oil.

8. Serve the toasted bread from a platter with the white bean puree alongside and a spoon for spreading.

GRILLED VEGETABLE AND JACK CHEESE SANDWICH

MAKES 4 SANDWICHES

A GRILLED VEGETABLE SANDWICH can be something truly special if it's made with green-market or garden-fresh vegetables. I enjoy adding some cheese for extra flavor and texture and also for the fun of fashioning a grilled cheese sandwich without the mess of cooking it. (The heat of the grilled vegetables warms the cheese.) If you've ever been frustrated by the soggy bread that seems part and parcel of grilled vegetable sandwiches, use an indestructible toasted baguette. For an impromptu lunch, serve this with a simple green salad and a platter of sliced, cured meat.

1 red bell pepper, stemmed, halved, and seeded, each half cut lengthwise into thirds

1 green zucchini (about 5 ounces), cut into long slices

1 Japanese eggplant (about 5 ounces), cut into long slices

¼ cup extra virgin olive oil

Fine sea salt and freshly ground black pepper

1 baguette (about 16 inches long)

4 ounces Jack or Colby cheese, cut into thin slices

¼ cup loosely packed basil

A few drops balsamic vinegar

Chopped herbs such as thyme, oregano, and flat-leaf parsley, optional

1. Prepare an outdoor grill for grilling, or preheat a grill pan over medium-high heat. Brush the pepper, zucchini, and eggplant lightly with oil, season with salt and pepper, and grill until well charred, 1 to 3 minutes per side, depending on the heat of the flame and its proximity to the grate. Remove the vegetables from the grill and let cool for a few minutes. Use a paring knife to remove any blackened skin from the peppers.

2. Meanwhile, slice the bread open lengthwise and brush the inside lightly with oil. Grill the cut side of the bread for a minute or so, just to

INSTEAD OF THE PEPPER,
ZUCCHINI, AND EGGPLANT,
use green or yellow bell peppers;
cored, quartered radicchio;
and/or yellow summer squash.

USE FRESH GOAT CHEESE or
mozzarella instead of Jack.

ADD THINLY SLICED
PROSCIUTTO to the sandwich
along with the cheese, especially
if substituting mozzarella.

heat it and give it some color. (If using a grill pan, you may need to halve the bread crosswise to fit it on the pan.)

3. Assemble the sandwich by alternating layers of vegetables, cheese, and basil in the center of the bread. Drizzle with any remaining oil and a few drops of vinegar. Sprinkle on any herbs, if using, then tightly wrap the loaf in sandwich paper; the heat of the vegetables will warm and soften the cheese. Slice the sandwich through the paper into 4-inch segments and serve warm.

OPEN-FACED SWORDFISH, PORTOBELLO, AND PANCETTA CLUB

MAKES 4 SANDWICHES

OPEN-FACED SANDWICHES LET you make something heftier than a conventional sandwich and still use a foundation of bread. For example, no two slices of bread could contain the swordfish and portobello mushrooms here and, even if they could, getting your mouth around it cleanly would be quite a challenge. Open-faced sandwiches signal the diner that this is a time to use a knife and fork and look at the bread not as a vehicle for picking up the other ingredients but rather as a way to soak up and enjoy all of the juices that would otherwise be left on the plate.

1 pound swordfish, cut into four ½-inch-thick steaks

4 large portobello mushroom caps, stems removed

Olive oil

Fine sea salt and freshly ground black pepper

2 tablespoons lemon zest plus 2 tablespoons freshly squeezed lemon juice

3 tablespoons chopped thyme

½ cup mayonnaise

¼ pound thinly sliced pancetta

Four ¾-inch-thick slices country bread

4 large leaves iceberg lettuce

2 avocados, thinly sliced

1 beefsteak tomato, seeded and thinly sliced

1. Brush the swordfish steaks and mushroom caps lightly with oil and season with salt and pepper. Stir the lemon zest and half the thyme leaves together in a small bowl. Sprinkle the mixture over the mushrooms.

2. Stir the mayonnaise, remaining thyme leaves, and lemon juice together in a bowl. Set aside.

3. Preheat a sauté pan over medium-high heat. Put in the pancetta and cook until crisp, about 5 minutes. Use tongs to set aside on a paper towel–lined plate.

INSTEAD OF SWORDFISH, use tuna or mahi mahi steaks, which will complement the other ingredients.

IF YOU CAN'T FIND PANCETTA, use thinly sliced, wood-smoked bacon.

4. Heat an outdoor grill or grill pan. Toast or grill the bread slices until golden. Put one slice on each of 4 dinner plates and set aside.

5. Grill the mushroom caps until they begin to brown, about 2 minutes, then turn over and cook on the other side for 2 minutes. Transfer to a plate and set aside.

6. Grill the swordfish steaks until cooked on the outside, but still medium-rare inside, 3 to 4 minutes per side. Remove the steaks from the grill.

7. Place a lettuce leaf on each piece of bread and top with sliced avocado, tomato, swordfish, mushroom, and pancetta. Drizzle lemon-thyme mayonnaise over the top and serve.

PHILLY CHEESE STEAK

MAKES 4 SANDWICHES

As much as any food can be associated with a city, Philadelphia is the provenance of cheese steaks. In countless eateries around the city you can order a hoagie of thinly sliced meat, gloriously gooey cheese, and a variety of other ingredients including onions, sweet and hot peppers, and tomato sauce. Cheese steaks aren't all that refined, but they are great, greasy fun. When I crave a cheese steak, I take it to a new level, using prime aged beef, imported Italian cheese, and an artisan-baked loaf of bread. If you like, you can flavor the beef's cooking oil by adding a whole, peeled garlic clove to the oil and browning it for a minute or two while cooking the beef.

1 pound shell, sirloin, or rib steak, well trimmed and boneless

About ¼ cup extra virgin olive oil

1 Vidalia or other sweet onion, halved and thinly sliced

Fine sea salt and freshly ground black pepper

4 to 6 Italian frying peppers, halved and stemmed, seeds discarded

4 soft hero breads or hoagie rolls, halved lengthwise

Balsamic vinegar

¼ pound imported fontina or sharp, aged provolone, thinly sliced

1. Slice the beef thinly on an electric meat slicer, or use the following method: with plastic wrap, tightly roll the steak into a torpedo or log shape. Put the beef log in the freezer for 30 to 45 minutes to firm it until tight *but not frozen*. Remove the plastic wrap and, working quickly, use an electric knife to slice the beef into paper-thin slices, almost shaving the beef. If this does not produce very thin results, cut the beef into the thinnest slices possible and flatten the slices using a meat pounder. Once all the beef has been cut, refrigerate until the remaining ingredients are ready.

2. Heat 2 tablespoons of the oil in a heavy-bottomed sauté pan set over low heat. Put in the onions, season with salt and pepper, and cook until

NIGHTLY
SPECIALS

USE THINLY SLICED CHICKEN
BREAST instead of beef.

USE FRESH MOZZARELLA
instead of fontina or provolone.

ADD SOME SLICED RED AND
YELLOW PEPPERS to the frying
peppers.

IF YOU LIKE IT SPICIER, add
some pickled jalapeño slices.

nicely softened and lightly caramelized but not browned, about 20 minutes. Transfer the onions to a bowl and set aside. Add the pepper halves to
the pan, season with salt and pepper, and fry until soft and tender, about
12 minutes. Transfer to the bowl with the onions. Keep the onions and
peppers covered and warm.

3. In a clean, heavy-bottomed sauté pan, heat the remaining oil over
medium heat. Add the beef in batches and lightly brown, seasoning with
salt and pepper as you cook, and adding more oil if necessary.

4. Pull out a little of the doughy insides of each loaf, then drizzle lightly
with oil, a splash of vinegar, and a pinch of salt and pepper. Put one-quarter
of the beef inside each roll, top with onions and peppers, and finish with
several slices of cheese. Wrap snugly in sandwich wrapping paper, slice
diagonally in half, and serve.

PIZZA BIANCA

MAKES 2 OR 3 PIZZAS

THIS PIZZA IS BASED ON one they make in the Campo de' Fiori marketplace in Rome which, despite its poetic name, is a nitty-gritty, inner-city, outdoor market. The pizzaioli (pizza makers or bakers known for breads and sweet things) there are famous for pizza bianca, or white pizza. The pizzaiola stretches the dough out to six or eight feet in length and a mere eight inches wide, then uses a wooden board to slide it into an equally lengthy white-hot oven to bake it. When it comes out, he sprinkles it with extra virgin olive oil and sea salt and cuts it into squares. Market-goers walk around munching on great slabs of this white pizza as a midmorning or midafternoon snack. Put it to the same use at parties: it makes a great snack before dinner or as part of a brunch. If you've never made pizza before, this gives you a chance to focus on little besides the dough itself.

All-purpose flour, for dusting

Pizza and Flatbread Dough (page 56)

¼ cup cornmeal

¼ cup extra virgin olive oil

Fine sea salt

1. Set a pizza stone on the center rack. Preheat the oven to 450°F, or higher if possible.

2. Sprinkle some flour on the work surface.

3. Divide the dough into halves or thirds, depending on how thin or thick you like your pizza. Work the dough, rolling it into a ball, then flattening it into a circle with the palm of your hand. Press with your fingertips from the center outward, widening the circle. Start pushing this small circle into an oblong or rectangular shape, always leveling the thickness of the dough, so that the dough is about 14 by 6 inches.

ADD INGREDIENTS that still let you appreciate the simplicity of this pizza: a scattering of thinly sliced hot chiles, crushed red pepper flakes, or diced tomato add flavor without overwhelming the pizza.

4.   Sprinkle some cornmeal on a pizza peel (the big wooden spatula on which pizza is moved around) or the underside of an overturned cookie sheet. Pick up the dough and, in one deft movement, transfer it to the cornmeal-dusted peel.

5.   Brush the dough lightly with oil and sprinkle with some salt.

6.   Pick up the peel and open the oven door. Gently slide the pizza onto the stone; a few shakes of the peel and the dough should slide right off, thanks to the cornmeal.

7.   Bake the pizza until the top is golden brown and the bottom is turning a dark, golden color and crisping nicely, 15 minutes or less. Use tongs to carefully slide the pizza back onto the peel to remove the pizza from the oven, brush it with more oil, cut into 2-inch-wide strips, and serve. While the first pizza is baking, ready the next one. Bake it as you enjoy the first one. Repeat until you've used all the dough and other ingredients.

PIZZA AND FLATBREAD DOUGH

MAKES ENOUGH DOUGH FOR TWO OR THREE 12-INCH PIZZA CRUSTS, DEPENDING ON THICKNESS

3 cups unbleached flour, plus more for dusting a work surface

Fine sea salt

1 envelope (¼ ounce) active dry yeast

3 tablespoons olive oil

1. Process the flour and 2 teaspoons salt in the bowl of a standing mixer fitted with the dough hook until thoroughly incorporated, 1 minute.

2. Put the yeast in another bowl. Whisk in ¼ cup warm water, then 2 tablespoons of the oil. Let rest until the liquid begins to foam, about 10 minutes, then pour this mixture into the center of the flour. Mix the flour and yeast solution until incorporated. Add ¾ cup warm water to the flour and mix again until the dough pulls together into a single, unified mass.

3. Turn the mass out onto a lightly floured surface and begin to knead the dough by working it with the heel of your hand. Push outward and pull the inside edge over the top. Repeat the process over and over to create a smooth ball of dough free of stickiness. This should take 6 to 8 minutes.

4. Brush a clean, stainless-steel bowl with the remaining tablespoon oil and put the ball of dough in the bowl. Cover with a clean cloth and let rise at room temperature until it has doubled in size, 1½ to 2 hours.

5. When the dough has risen, divide it in half, or thirds for thinner pizzas, and shape the pieces into balls that will later be patted into the traditional pizza shape. The balls of dough can be individually wrapped in plastic and frozen for up to 2 months.

FLATBREAD WITH SAUSAGE, BELL PEPPERS, AND ASIAGO

MAKES 2 OR 3 FLATBREADS, DEPENDING ON THICKNESS

THERE'S NO TOMATO OR MOZZARELLA on this *flatbread.*
Instead, we have sausage, sweet bell peppers, and Asiago cheese, just one example of how you can devise a simple but original pizza by drawing on just a handful of ingredients.

All-purpose flour, for dusting a work surface

Pizza and Flatbread Dough (page 56)

Cornmeal

2 to 3 tablespoons extra virgin olive oil

1 pound Asiago or Parmigiano-Reggiano, shaved

½ pound Italian sausage, casings removed, meat crumbled into nut-size nuggets

1 red bell pepper, stemmed, seeded, and cut into thin strips

1. Set a pizza stone on the center rack. Preheat the oven to 450°F, or higher if possible.

2. Sprinkle some flour on the work surface.

3. Divide the dough into halves or thirds, depending on how thin or thick you like your flatbread. Work the dough, rolling it into a ball, then flattening it into a circle with the palm of your hand. Press with your fingertips from the center outward, widening the circle. Start pushing this small circle into an oblong or rectangular shape, always leveling the thickness of the dough, so that the dough is about 14 by 6 inches.

4. Sprinkle some cornmeal on a pizza peel or the underside of a cookie sheet. Pick up the dough and, in one deft movement, transfer it to the peel.

5. Drizzle 1 tablespoon of the olive oil over the surface of the flatbread. Sprinkle half (or one-third if making three flatbreads) of the Asiago evenly over the dough and then scatter one-half or one-third (if making three flatbreads) of the sausage and pepper over the surface.

REPLACE THE BELL PEPPER with a hot chile.

USE ROBIOLA OR TALEGGIO instead of Asiago.

REPLACE THE SAUSAGE with browned ground beef, sliced meatballs, or diced leftover chicken or turkey.

6. Pick up the peel and open the oven door. Gently slide the flatbread onto the stone; a few shakes of the peel and the dough should slide right off, thanks to the cornmeal.

7. Bake the flatbread until the surface is bubbling and the bottom of the crust is turning a dark, golden color and crisping nicely, 15 minutes or less. Use the peel to remove the flatbread from the oven, cut it into slices, and serve. While the first flatbread is baking, ready the next one. Bake it as you enjoy the first one. Repeat until you've used all the dough and other ingredients.

SUPER

Soups, Chowders, and Stews

BOWLS

The concept of soup du jour seems so quaint and old-fashioned that it's easy to overlook the fact that it was one of the first incarnations of the nightly special. Daily soup specials allow the cook to scour the kitchen and market and let the mood, inventory, season, and inspiration of the day dictate what goes into the pot. In other words, soups reflect the thoughtfulness of the cook.

This chapter is devoted to soups and their close relatives, chowders and stews. Soups and chowders are a part of a broad category with many subgenres. For our purposes, soup is differentiated from chowder by its sheer weight: chowder is chockful of ingredients while soup is lighter, with fewer bits of vegetables, meat, and fish. While both soups and chowders might serve as either a first course or a light meal, stew is definitely a main event. I think of the soup and stew pot as a place to create foolproof specials, because the fundamental technique for making them is essentially the same: begin by cooking some meat, fish, or vegetables with herbs and spices, add some stock or broth, and let it simmer.

Stews and braised dishes like lamb shanks are a lot alike; they both feature relatively modest and affordable ingredients. Both benefit from longer cooking times to tenderize the tougher cuts of meat whose best flavors take time to draw out. I make extra and save the leftovers and enjoy an encore serving the next day, when they are likely to taste even better. In fact, miraculously, the leftovers might just be the best part of the deal. Now, that's special!

CURRIED PEA SOUP WITH FRIZZLED GINGER

SERVES 6 TO 8

PEA SOUP IS ONE OF THE EASIEST, most spontaneous ways to take advantage of seasonal ingredients. Just-picked peas taste of spring and early summer with their fresh green flavor and gentle sweetness. Because their sugars begin to turn to starch after they've been picked, peas have a very limited shelf life. Buy peas only from farmers' markets or independent markets that get their produce from local farmers.

If you don't have any stock on hand, don't worry: this dish will be delicious even if it's made with water. It's also great chilled, so prepared it as soon as you get home from the market and save it for a day or two in the fridge if you won't have occasion to eat it right away.

If peas are not in season don't use frozen peas. Instead, turn to another common seasonal vegetable like asparagus or sugar snap peas.

2 tablespoons unsalted butter

1 small onion, cut into small dice

1 celery stalk, cut into small dice

1 leek (white part only), well washed, quartered, and thinly sliced crosswise

Fine sea salt and freshly ground black pepper

2 teaspoons curry powder

2 quarts homemade vegetable stock (page 65) or low-sodium, store-bought vegetable broth simmering in a pot over low heat on a back burner

Herb sachet of 2 bay leaves and 4 thyme sprigs, tied in cheesecloth

3 cups fresh shelled peas (from about 2½ pounds peas in the pod)

1 cup crème fraîche (see page 64) or sour cream

Frizzled Ginger (page 66)

1. Melt the butter in a large, heavy-bottomed pot over medium-high heat. Add the onion, celery, and leek and season with salt and pepper. Sauté the vegetables until they are softened but not browned, about 5 minutes. Add the curry powder, stir, and cook for 2 more minutes.

2. Add the stock and herb sachet to the pot. Bring to a boil over high heat, then lower the heat and let simmer until the vegetables have completely softened, 10 to 12 minutes. Add the peas and simmer for an additional 10 minutes.

3. Use tongs to remove and discard the herb sachet.

4. Use an immersion blender to puree the soup in the pot, or puree it in batches in a standing blender, then return the soup to the pot over medium heat. Stir in the crème fraîche, being careful not to let the soup return to a boil. (If you like, reserve a few tablespoons of the crème fraîche to drizzle over each serving.)

5. Divide the soup among individual bowls and serve at once, topping each serving with a drizzle of crème fraîche, if desired, and a few pieces of frizzled ginger.

Crème fraîche

Crème fraîche is a lighter style of French cream that has been "inoculated," like sour cream. It's often available from specialty stores, where you'll find it in the dairy or cheese section. It has an appealing tang and thickening ability with less fat than butter. In this recipe, it helps maintain the fresh quality of the soup. If you can't find it, either heavy cream or sour cream is generally a viable substitute.

YOUR NIGHTLY SPECIALS

REPLACE THE CURRY POWDER with ancho chile powder or stir in some fresh thyme leaves at the end.

TURN THIS INTO A LUNCH OR BRUNCH DISH by adding diced, cooked lobster meat, crabmeat, or poached shrimp just moments before serving. Or serve the soup chilled and finish it by adding chilled, cooked shellfish. Chilled leftover chicken can also be diced and added.

INSTEAD OF BEGINNING WITH BUTTER, warm ½ cup diced pancetta or bacon in the pot. When it has rendered enough fat to coat the bottom of the pot, add the onion, celery, and leeks and proceed. Use only ½ cup crème fraîche and leave out the curry powder and frizzled ginger.

VEGETABLE STOCK

MAKES ABOUT 5 QUARTS

½ cup olive oil

2 large Spanish onions, quartered

½ head celery, roughly chopped

1 large leek, split, well washed, and cut into large pieces

2 large carrots, peeled and roughly chopped

One 15.5-ounce can crushed tomatoes

1 cup sliced button mushrooms

1 pound Idaho or russet potatoes, quartered

5 flat-leaf parsley sprigs

4 thyme sprigs

2 garlic cloves, smashed

½ teaspoon fine sea salt

½ teaspoon black peppercorns

2 whole cloves

1. Pour the oil into a heavy-bottomed stockpot over medium heat. Add all the other ingredients and cook, stirring, over medium-low heat until the vegetables have softened but not colored, about 15 minutes. Pour in 6 quarts water, raise the heat to high, and bring the water to a boil, then lower the heat and let the liquid simmer for 2 hours.

2. Carefully strain the stock through a fine-mesh strainer set over a large bowl or pot, pressing down on the solids with a wooden spoon to extract as much liquid and flavor as possible. Let the stock cool, then refrigerate for up to 1 week or freeze in batches to be thawed and used as needed.

FRIZZLED GINGER

Serve these crispy strands of ginger as a garnish for Coconut-Scented Basmati Rice (page 97), Curried Wheat Berries with Sweet Onions (page 108), Pan-Fried Grouper with Papaya Relish and Chili Oil (page 150), or Braised Chicken with Butternut Squash, Walnuts, and Sage (page 180), as well as other soups and salads, especially those featuring Asian ingredients like cilantro and ginger.

1 cup vegetable oil

1 knob ginger (about 4 ounces), peeled

Fine sea salt

1. Pour the oil into a small pot and heat to 265°F over medium-high heat. (Clip a thermometer to the side of the pot.)

2. While the oil is heating up, shave the ginger into a fine julienne using a Japanese mandoline, vegetable slicer, or very sharp, thin-bladed knife.

3. When the oil has reached the desired temperature, add the ginger in small batches, frying them until crispy, about 1 minute; use a slotted spoon to remove them to a paper towel–lined plate to drain. Salt each batch as soon as it hits the paper. These crisps can be held at room temperature for up to 2 hours.

ROASTED EGGPLANT AND ELEPHANT GARLIC SOUP

SERVES 4 TO 6

THE FIRST TIME I served this soup was at '21' in 1987, when I whipped it up as a special to use elephant garlic, which was all the rage at the time. Though a brilliant marketing ploy, using the name elephant garlic wasn't really truth in advertising, because it isn't garlic. This Oregon-grown, white-skinned vegetable is more likely a wild ancestor of the leek. Its bulbs are large, sometimes up to one pound. Minced or roasted in sauces and soups, it contributes a distinctly gentle sweetness. If you can't find it, use "regular" garlic instead.

1 large, firm eggplant (about 2 pounds), halved lengthwise, skin intact

½ cup olive oil

Fine sea salt and freshly ground black pepper

1 large red bell pepper, stemmed, seeded, and chopped

2 large onions, chopped

3 carrots, peeled and chopped

2 celery stalks, roughly chopped

1 cup canned tomatoes, drained of their juice

6 elephant garlic cloves or 12 regular garlic cloves

3 quarts homemade chicken stock (page 69), low-sodium, store-bought chicken broth, or water

1 teaspoon ground cumin

6 thyme sprigs

6 rosemary sprigs

2 bay leaves

¼ teaspoon cayenne pepper

Thinly shaved pecorino Romano

1. Preheat the oven to 375°F.

2. Brush the exposed flesh of the eggplant generously with some of the oil and season it with salt and pepper. Set aside.

3. Put the peppers, onions, carrots, celery, tomatoes, and garlic in a roasting pan, drizzle with the remaining oil, and season with salt and pepper. Add the eggplant, skin side up, and spread the vegetables out in a single

layer. Roast until the eggplant turns mushy in its skin, about 45 minutes, stirring and shaking the pan occasionally to prevent scorching and to make sure the vegetables cook evenly.

4.   When the vegetables are done, use tongs to remove and set aside the eggplant to cool for a few minutes. Transfer the remaining vegetables to a large, heavy-bottomed pot. Add the stock and bring to a boil over high heat. Using a large spoon, scoop out the eggplant flesh, discard the skin, and add the roasted eggplant to the pot. Add the cumin, thyme, rosemary, bay leaves, and cayenne and season with salt and pepper. Lower the heat and let the soup simmer until all of the vegetables are tender enough to puree, about 30 minutes.

5.   Use an immersion blender to puree the soup in the pot, or puree it in batches in a standing blender, then return the soup to the pot over medium heat.

6.   Divide the soup among 4 to 6 bowls and serve, passing the shaved pecorino alongside and inviting everyone to top his or her serving with cheese. If you prefer, you may also serve the soup chilled.

YOUR NIGHTLY SPECIALS

REPLACE THE EGGPLANT with a large dice of zucchini. Or make a sweet bell pepper soup by leaving out the eggplant and using a total of 4 peppers.

INSTEAD OF CAYENNE AND CUMIN, use more thyme and rosemary and add a few sprigs of oregano for Mediterranean-style soup.

RATHER THAN PUREEING THE EGGPLANT, chop it after roasting, and return it to the soup.

STRAIN ANY EXTRA SOUP through a fine-mesh strainer, whisk in a few tablespoons of white wine vinegar, lemon juice, or olive oil and use it as a sauce for grilled chicken or fish.

CHICKEN STOCK
MAKES ABOUT 4 QUARTS

8 pounds chicken bones, soaked in several changes of cold water and drained

3 large carrots, peeled and roughly chopped

2 large onions, roughly chopped

4 celery stalks, chopped

2 leeks, split, well washed, and roughly chopped

3 thyme sprigs

2 bay leaves

3 garlic cloves, smashed

1 tablespoon fine sea salt

1 tablespoon black peppercorns

1.   Put all of the ingredients in a pot and pour in 6 quarts water. Bring the water to a boil over high heat, then lower the heat and let the liquid simmer for 4 hours. Periodically skim any impurities that rise to the surface.

2.   Carefully strain the stock through a fine-mesh strainer set over a large bowl or pot, pressing down on the solids with a wooden spoon to extract as much liquid and flavor as possible. Let the stock cool, then use a spoon to skim off any fat that rises to the surface. Refrigerate for up to 1 week or freeze in batches to be thawed and used as needed.

ROASTED CORN CHOWDER WITH SHRIMP AND TARRAGON

MAKES 1½ QUARTS CHOWDER, SERVING 4 TO 6

For me, corn chowder is an annual rite of passage that marks the point when summer begins to turn to fall. To savor this too-short taste of summer, I try to get as much seasonal flavor as possible into the bowl by grilling or roasting the corn and adding shrimp or other shellfish. This is a very chunky chowder, full of vegetables, yet in a light broth. It also features a mysterious hint of flavor provided by an unexpected ingredient: vanilla.

4 ears fresh sweet corn, shucked

3 tablespoons unsalted butter

Fine sea salt and freshly ground black pepper

6 cups homemade chicken stock (page 69) or low-sodium, store-bought chicken broth

1 large onion, diced (about 1 cup)

2 celery stalks, diced

1 leek, split, well washed, and thinly sliced crosswise

1 large red bell pepper, stemmed, seeded, and diced

1 jalapeño pepper, seeded and diced

1 teaspoon ground coriander

Seeds from 1 vanilla bean

¼ teaspoon cayenne pepper

1 pound medium shrimp, peeled and deveined, cut in half lengthwise

1 cup heavy cream

2 tablespoons chopped tarragon

1. Prepare an outdoor grill for grilling or preheat the broiler.

2. Brush the corncobs with about 1 tablespoon of the butter and season them with salt and pepper. Grill or broil them on a cookie sheet, turning until toasted all over, about 10 minutes total cooking time. Set the cobs aside and let them cool. When cool enough to handle, stand the cobs on end and draw a chef's knife down along the cobs to remove the kernels. You should have about 2½ cups kernels. Set the kernels and cobs aside separately.

YOU CAN USE OTHER SHELL-FISH, OR EVEN FISH, INSTEAD OF SHRIMP. Some suggestions:

1 lobster, 1¼ pounds, split and broiled or grilled, shelled, meat cut into 1-inch dice

¼ pound fresh crabmeat or

½ pound diced monkfish, poached in the chowder during the last 6 to 8 minutes of cooking

3. Pour the stock into a pot and warm it over medium heat. Put the remaining 2 tablespoons butter in a separate large, heavy-bottomed pot and set the pot over medium heat. Add the onion, celery, leek, bell pepper, and jalapeño and sauté until the vegetables are softened but not browned, about 6 minutes. Add the cumin, coriander, vanilla, cayenne, and 1 teaspoon of salt, stir well, and cook until the mixture becomes nicely fragrant, 2 to 3 minutes. Pour in the hot broth, raise the heat to high, and bring it to a boil. Add the corncobs to punch up the corn flavor and, when the liquid returns to a boil, lower the heat until it is just simmering. Continue to simmer for 40 minutes.

4. Use tongs or a slotted spoon to remove and discard the cobs. Add the shrimp, cream, and corn kernels and cook until the shrimp are firm and pink, about 4 minutes.

5. Ladle the chowder into individual bowls. Garnish with the tarragon and serve.

CUBAN-STYLE BLACK BEAN SOUP

SERVES 6 TO 8

BLACK BEAN SOUP crosses many oceans and borders and is popular in a number of cultures around the world, each of which has adapted it to include its own indigenous ingredients. Most people, however, associate black bean soup with Cuban cooking, the direction taken here with smoked ham hock, cumin, and rum.

1 pound dried black (turtle) beans, picked over for dirt or debris

3 tablespoons olive oil

1 smoked ham hock, or other smoked ham product

3 medium white onions, chopped (about 1½ cups)

2 large red bell peppers, stemmed, seeded, and chopped

3 celery stalks, chopped

2 tablespoons chili powder

1 tablespoon ground cumin

2 tablespoons minced garlic

¼ cup tomato paste

Fine sea salt and freshly ground black pepper

⅓ cup light rum

Sour cream

Chopped scallions or chives

1. Rinse the beans in cold water, drain them, put in a bowl, cover by 1 inch with cold water, and let soak in the refrigerator overnight. (Alternatively, you can quick-soak the beans by covering them with water in a pot. Bring to a boil over high heat, then cover the pot and turn off the heat. Let the beans soak until tender, 1 to 2 hours.)

2. When ready to make the soup, drain the beans and set them aside.

3. Pour the oil into a large, heavy-bottomed pot and set it over medium heat. When the oil is hot but not smoking, add the ham hock, onions, peppers, celery, chili powder, and cumin. Sauté until the vegetables are softened but not browned, about 6 minutes. Add the garlic and tomato paste and cook for an additional 3 minutes, stirring to make sure you don't scorch the tomato or garlic.

SPOON SOME STORE-BOUGHT SALSA into the center of each bowl, or use the Corn Salsa on page 141.

FINISH THE SOUP by stirring in a teaspoon or more of Tabasco or other hot sauce.

FOR A THICKER SOUP, or to serve black beans as a side dish, puree just a portion of the soup, or none at all. If serving as a side dish, steam some white rice, the traditional accompaniment, and serve it on the side.

FOR A FUN, INTERACTIVE MEAL, set out small bowls or ramekins full of garnishes like chili sauce, sour cream, salsa, chopped chives, and a plate of warm flour tortillas, and let diners doctor their soup to taste.

A FEW TABLESPOONS OF THE SOUP can be used as a sauce for roasted pork or chicken.

4.   Pour 4 quarts water into the pot, raise the heat to high, and bring to a boil. Add the beans to the pot, stir, and when the water returns to a boil, lower the heat and let simmer until the beans are tender but still holding their shape, 2 to 2½ hours.

5.   Remove the pot from the heat and season the soup with salt and pepper. Use tongs to remove the ham hock and set it aside to cool. The beans are like molten lava at this point and ready to explode, so let them cool for 10 to 15 minutes, then puree with an immersion blender or in small batches in a standing blender. When the hock is cool enough to handle, pick off the meat and set it aside. The soup and meat can be cooled, covered, and refrigerated separately for up to 1 week.

6.   When ready to serve, return the soup to a boil and add the rum and ham. Cook for 2 minutes more.

7.   Ladle the soup into 6 to 8 bowls and garnish each serving with a tablespoon of sour cream and a scattering of scallions.

CHICKEN POT PIE

SERVES 6

For today's cooks, especially in the age of rediscovered comfort food, pot pies (stews with a crust) are an invitation to use inventive combinations. I've made lobster, fish, game, and other types of pot pies, seasoned with everything from chile peppers to curry powder to star anise. Pot pies are a classic, free-form vehicle for favorite ingredients. Think of this recipe, which uses exotic mushrooms and tarragon, as a blank canvas. Best of all, the rustic presentation in individual crocks has no bottom crust, just a biscuit topping. The topping can be made (but not baked) and refrigerated for up to three days, or frozen for up to two weeks. Similarly, the chicken and broth (steps 4 and 5) can be made and refrigerated separately for up to two days.

2½ cups sifted all-purpose unbleached flour, plus more for dusting a work surface

2 tablespoons sugar

1 tablespoon baking powder

Fine sea salt and freshly ground black pepper

¾ cup buttermilk

1¼ cups heavy cream

8 tablespoons (1 stick) cold

unsalted butter, cut into small pieces, plus 1 tablespoon melted butter and 1 tablespoon at room temperature

One 3- to 3½-pound chicken

2 bay leaves

1 teaspoon black peppercorns

2 teaspoons dried rosemary

2 teaspoons dried thyme

1 large onion, studded with

6 cloves

5 large carrots, peeled and diced

4 celery stalks, diced

1 leek, well washed and diced

2 tablespoons minced shallots

1 pound mixed exotic mushrooms such as chanterelle, oyster, and cremini, sliced or broken up by hand

¼ cup chopped tarragon

1.   Make the pot pie tops: In the bowl of a mixer fitted with the paddle attachment, combine the flour, sugar, baking powder, and ½ teaspoon salt. After the dry ingredients are thoroughly blended, add the buttermilk and ¼ cup of the cream and paddle until well incorporated. Add the cold butter pieces in rapid succession, paddling only briefly, to leave the mixture as mealy as possible.

2. Scrape the lumpy dough onto a lightly floured board and flatten gently with a rolling pin into a rectangle about 1 inch thick. Cut into six 3-inch rounds.

3. Brush a cookie sheet lightly with the melted butter, place the rounds on the sheet, and place the cookie sheet in the refrigerator to rest for 20 minutes, while you preheat the oven to 375°F. Bake the chilled rounds for 20 to 25 minutes, until they are nicely browned. Remove from the oven and set aside. While they are baking, begin the chicken.

4. Make the chicken and broth: wash the chicken under cold running water and pat dry with paper towels. Tie the bay leaves, peppercorns, rosemary, and thyme together in a piece of cheesecloth as a bouquet garni. Put the chicken into a pot large enough to hold it, cover with cold water, and bring to a boil over medium-high heat. Reduce to a simmer and cook for

THE CHARACTER AND FLAVOR of this pot pie have almost count-less variations. You can use a combination of parsley, marjoram, sage, and/or tarragon in place of the rosemary and thyme.

REPLACE THE MUSHROOMS with spring and summer vegetables like peas (either fresh or high-quality frozen *petits pois*), asparagus, and/or morels.

TO CREATE A NEWFANGLED SHEPHERD'S PIE, top the crocks with mashed potatoes rather than pastry rounds.

USE LEFTOVER ROAST TURKEY or roast beef in place of chicken. If using beef, substitute beef broth for chicken broth.

15 minutes, carefully skimming off any impurities that accumulate on the surface. Add 2 teaspoons salt, the bouquet garni, onion, half the carrots, half the celery, and the leek. When the water returns to a boil, reduce to a persistent simmer and cook, uncovered, for 45 minutes.

5. While the chicken is cooking, fill a large bowl with ice water. When the chicken is done, remove it from the pot and cool it by lowering it into the ice water. As it cools, strain the broth into a 4-quart pot or casserole, reserving 2 cups of it. (Discard the solids; save the remaining broth for another use.) When the chicken is thoroughly cold, strip off and discard all of the skin. Strip the meat from the bones and shred, using scrupulously clean hands and an immaculate work station.

6. Make the mushroom and tarragon sauce: bring the chicken broth to a boil over high heat. Add the remaining carrots and celery and simmer for 10 minutes.

7. Meanwhile, melt the remaining 1 tablespoon butter in a sauté pan set over medium heat, add the shallots, and sauté them. After 3 minutes, add the mushrooms to the pan, raise the heat, and cook for 5 minutes. Season with ½ teaspoon salt and ½ teaspoon black pepper.

8. To the pot with the chicken broth and vegetables, add the remaining 1 cup cream, then add the sautéed mushrooms and shallots. Allow to simmer for 5 minutes, then add the chicken meat. Cook for 20 minutes, add the tarragon, and transfer to 6 crocks. During the last 5 minutes, reheat the pastry rounds in a nonstick pan in a 200°F oven for 2 to 3 minutes. Top each crock with a pastry round and serve at once.

QUICK POT PIE

SERVES 6

This alternate recipe uses leftover roasted chicken, prepared stock, and frozen puff pastry for a much quicker preparation. It's just one example of why, when roasting chicken, I always roast an extra one: there's so much you can do with it the next day!

3 cups homemade chicken stock (page 69) or low-sodium, store-bought chicken broth

2 large carrots, peeled and diced

2 celery stalks, diced

1 tablespoon unsalted butter, at room temperature

2 tablespoons minced shallots

1 pound mixed exotic mushrooms such as chanterelle, oyster, or cremini, sliced or broken up by hand

½ teaspoon coarse salt

½ teaspoon freshly ground black pepper

1 package frozen puff pastry, thawed to room temperature

1 tablespoon unsalted butter, melted

1 cup heavy cream

2 to 3 cups cubed, cold roasted chicken

¼ cup chopped tarragon

1. Bring the chicken stock to a boil in a heavy-bottomed, 4-quart pot or casserole over high heat. Add the carrots and celery, lower the heat, and simmer for 10 minutes.

2. Meanwhile, melt the 1 tablespoon room temperature butter in a sauté pan set over medium heat, add the shallots, and sauté them. After 3 minutes, add the mushrooms to the pan, raise the heat, and cook for 5 minutes. Season with the salt and black pepper. Add more to taste if desired.

3. Preheat the oven to 375°F.

4. Use a biscuit cutter or a glass to cut the puff pastry into six 3-inch rounds. Brush a cookie sheet lightly with the melted butter, place the rounds on the sheet, and bake for 12 minutes, or until they are nicely browned. Remove and reserve.

5. To the pot with the broth and vegetables, add the cream, sautéed mushrooms, and shallots. Allow to simmer for 5 minutes, then add the chicken. Cook for 20 minutes, add the tarragon, and transfer to 6 crocks. Top each with a pastry round and serve at once.

BEEF AND PORTER STEW

SERVES 6 TO 8

THERE ARE DISHES YOU MAKE because the ingredients are in season and there are dishes you make because of the season. This is an example of the latter, a hearty, restorative stew that recalls Belgian cuisine with its combination of beef and dark beer, specifically porter, which is not as dark as stout. Porters have a sweetness and near-chocolate flavor from toasted barley that complements the beef very well. This stew is simple and humble but full of rich flavor. Serve this with Savory Chipotle Chile Muffins (page 246).

¼ cup vegetable oil

2 tablespoons unsalted butter

2 pounds beef stew meat or bottom round, cut into 1-inch cubes

Fine sea salt and freshly ground black pepper

1 onion, diced (about 1 cup)

¼ cup all-purpose flour

One 12-ounce bottle porter beer

2 cups low-sodium, store-bought beef broth, diluted with 2 cups water

Bouquet garni of 2 bay leaves, 4 thyme sprigs, and 4 rosemary sprigs tied in a cheesecloth bundle

½ cup canned, crushed tomatoes

½ cup carrots peeled and cut into small dice

½ cup celery cut into small dice

1 cup rutabaga (wax turnips), cut into small dice

1 cup parsnips cut into small dice

1.   Heat the oil and butter in a large, heavy-bottomed pot over medium-high heat. Season the beef with salt and pepper. Add the beef to the pot in a single, not-too-tightly-packed layer and brown the beef well on all sides, about 8 minutes total. Transfer the beef to a plate and set aside.

2.   Add the onion to the casserole and cook until golden and caramelized, about 15 minutes. Sprinkle the onion with the flour and stir to combine well.

3.   Return the beef to the casserole, pour in the porter and broth, and add the bouquet garni, tomatoes, 2 teaspoons salt, and 2 teaspoons pepper.

USE LAMB STEW MEAT instead.

OTHER BEERS, from light to dark, can be used to alter the character of the stew. Or use red wine instead.

Add the carrots, celery, rutabaga, and parsnips. Bring the liquid to a boil over high heat, then lower the heat and let simmer for 1 hour. Pick out and discard the bouquet garni.

4.   The stew can be made up to 2 days ahead, cooled, covered, and refrigerated. Reheat gently before serving.

MOROCCAN LAMB STEW

MAKES 3 QUARTS STEW, ENOUGH TO SERVE 4 TO 6 AS A MAIN COURSE

TAGINE IS THE NAME given to Moroccan dishes cooked in a domed, ceramic vessel which is also called a tagine. As the food bakes, the vessel captures the steam from the cooking ingredients, then returns it to the cooking liquid. If you don't own a tagine, a Dutch oven simulates the effect.

1 tablespoon ground coriander

1 tablespoon ground cumin

1 tablespoon ground turmeric

1½ teaspoons ground cardamom

¼ cup olive oil

3 pounds lamb shoulder, trimmed of excess fat, cut into 1-inch chunks

Fine sea salt and freshly ground black pepper

2 large red onions, halved and thinly sliced

4 carrots, peeled and cut into small dice

2 large leeks, white parts only, well washed, quartered, and thinly sliced crosswise

1 cup diced dried apricots

½ cup seeded diced dates

2 tablespoons chopped rosemary

2 tablespoons chopped oregano

2 tablespoons chopped mint

2 tablespoons chopped cilantro

½ teaspoon crushed red pepper flakes

¼ cup freshly squeezed lemon juice

One 15.5-ounce can plum tomatoes, drained of their liquid

One 10-ounce package quick-cooking couscous (about 1½ cups)

1. Stir the coriander, cumin, turmeric, and cardamom together in a large bowl to make a spice mix.

2. Heat the olive oil in a Dutch oven or large, heavy-bottomed casserole over low heat. Add the lamb chunks to the bowl with the spice mix and turn to coat the lamb well. Add the spice-coated lamb to the Dutch oven in batches, browning the pieces over low heat, taking care not to burn the spices. Season with salt and pepper.

3. Add the onions, carrots, and leeks to the pot and stir to combine well. Pour in enough water to come halfway up the lamb (about 2 quarts), raise

USE CHICKEN, or leave it out and make this with just vegetables.

ADD GOLDEN RAISINS, plumped in hot water for 10 minutes, to the couscous.

SERVE THE STEW over warm pita bread.

the heat to high, and bring it to a boil. Lower the heat and braise the lamb in the spiced broth until the meat is fork-tender, about 1½ hours. Add the apricots and dates.

4.   Meanwhile, process the rosemary, oregano, mint, cilantro, and pepper flakes together in a food processor. Add the lemon juice and tomatoes and pulse to a salsa-like consistency. Transfer the sauce to a small bowl.

5.   About 10 minutes before the stew is done, cook the couscous according to package directions. Or put the couscous in a bowl and pour just enough boiling water into the bowl to cover the couscous. Add a pinch of salt, stir once, cover with plastic wrap, and let steam until the couscous has absorbed the liquid, about 5 minutes. Remove the plastic and fluff the couscous with a fork.

6.   Remove the stew from the heat and stir in the herb-tomato mixture.

7.   Mound some couscous in the center of each of 4 to 6 wide soup plates or dinner plates. Top with some stew and serve hot.

TRUE

Pasta and Grains

GRITS

Pasta no longer belongs only to Italy. No matter where you go, you can find pasta dishes that have no relationship to Italian food. We have so thoroughly adopted pasta that it has become an all-American standby. When it comes to menu planning, pastas are a moveable piece: many of the pastas in this chapter can be an appetizer or main course, although a few should only be an appetizer, and one or two are rich enough that they should only be main courses.

Whether fresh or dried, cooked pasta should always have a slight bite. Dried pasta is hard and brittle; you can control the cooking time to keep it as al dente (toothsome) as you like. To determine doneness, remove a piece of pasta and look at its core. If it's not quite cooked enough, it will be white at the center, meaning you're eating raw dough. It should not be overcooked, however. Even fresh pasta should have a certain chewy quality when cooked.

Many grains are largely forgotten staples that can brighten up the table. Nightly specials can be anything that takes us on a new path: cooking barley, wheat berries, and quinoa might be the farthest thing from your mind, but they're all so easy to make that you should think of them as a way to turn even a simple roasted chicken dinner into something special with a quick but compelling side dish, which—if your schedule is anything like mine—can be a real life-saver once in a while.

FETTUCCINE WITH MUSHROOMS AND ASPARAGUS

SERVES 6 TO 8 AS AN APPETIZER OR 4 AS A MAIN COURSE

HERE'S A VERY SIMPLE TRICK *for making pasta dishes as delicious as possible: cook them in the classic Italian fashion by adding almost-cooked, drained pasta to the pan or pot with the sauce and letting it finish cooking there. Instead of swelling with more salted water during the final minutes, it'll drink in as much flavor as possible, in this case, the potent essence of sautéed mushrooms, red onion, cream, and herbs.*

Fine sea salt and freshly ground black pepper

¼ cup extra virgin olive oil

¼ cup red onion cut into small dice

¼ teaspoon crushed red pepper flakes, plus more to taste

½ pound cremini mushrooms, wiped clean with a damp cloth and thinly sliced

½ cup homemade vegetable stock (page 65) or store-bought, low-sodium vegetable broth

½ pound thin or pencil asparagus, thinly sliced on the bias, tip end left about 1½ inches long

¾ cup heavy cream

3 tablespoons pine nuts

1 pound dried fettuccine or pappardelle

2 tablespoons shredded basil

3 tablespoons unsalted butter

¼ cup freshly grated Parmigiano-Reggiano

1. Bring 6 quarts water to a boil in a large, heavy-bottomed pot over high heat, then add 2 tablespoons salt.

2. While waiting for the water to boil, heat the oil in a sauté pan over medium heat. Add the onion and pepper flakes and sauté quickly to keep the ingredients from scorching. Add the mushrooms, season with salt and pepper, and sauté until the mushrooms darken slightly in color and are softened but still holding their shape, about 5 minutes. Add the broth and asparagus and cook, stirring gently, for 2 minutes. Stir in the cream, immediately reduce the heat to keep it from scorching, and cook for several minutes.

3. Meanwhile, toast the pine nuts in a sauté pan over low heat, shaking the pan, just until they are warm and fragrant, about 2 minutes.

4. Add the pasta to the boiling water and cook until al dente, 7 to 9 minutes from the time the water returns to a boil (10 minutes if you are using pappardelle).

5. Add the basil, butter, pine nuts, and cheese to the pan with the mushrooms and toss well.

6. Reserve a cup or so of the pasta's cooking liquid, then drain the pasta and add it to the pan with the mushrooms, asparagus, and sauce. If the sauce seems too dry, stir in a few tablespoons of reserved pasta water. Toss, taste, and adjust the seasoning with salt, pepper, and more pepper flakes if necessary.

7. Present the pasta in a bowl and serve family style from the center of the table, or divide among individual plates.

YOUR NIGHTLY SPECIALS

MUSHROOMS: Instead of using the cremini, use 1 cup dried porcini mushrooms.

DRIED MUSHROOMS: Dried mushrooms like porcini, morel, and chanterelle offer a quick way to add flavor to cooking and are especially useful in the off season or winter months. Always rinse dried mushrooms under cold running water to remove any lingering dirt and sand, then reconstitute them in hot water for 20 minutes, drain, and strain the liquid. Save the liquid for soups and sauces. Keeping a small packet of dried mushrooms, which cost just a few dollars, in your pantry will give earthy flavor on demand.

USE A SPICE GRINDER to grind dried porcini to a powder. This seasoning powder will very economically make a full pot of risotto taste like a much more costly version, something many restaurants do to make flavors pop. Add 1 tablespoon to the finished mushrooms for a powerful and full flavor at an economical price.

PORCINI MUSHROOMS: Fresh porcini are among the most delicious of mushrooms. When they are available each fall, by all means use them, although they are expensive and need to be cooked as quickly as possible because they are highly perishable.

ADD ½ CUP OF BLANCHED AND SHOCKED FRESH OR FROZEN PEAS, spinach, and/or broccoli buds.

TOSS SOME SHREDDED, LEFT-OVER ROASTED TURKEY or duck meat into the pan along with the cooked pasta.

ALPINE BAKED PASTA

SERVES 6 TO 8 AS A MAIN COURSE

My FIRST JOB out of cooking school was working for a team of Swiss chefs. They loved pasta, especially with rich sauces. One recipe they adored featured pasta and potatoes tossed with a cheesy cream sauce. Through our nightly staff, or "family," meals, I became familiar with some of their high-altitude, rustic cooking.

This recipe combines two favorites of my Italian-American upbringing—macaroni and cheese and baked ziti—in the style of my Swiss mentors. It's included here for two reasons: first, it's a delicious, full-flavored dish, a one-pot pasta with a crunchy crust. Second, it demonstrates how you can bring your personal experiences into the kitchen.

4 tablespoons (½ stick) unsalted butter, plus more for the dish

Fine sea salt and freshly ground black pepper

2 tablespoons chopped sage

1 tablespoon poppy seeds

1 pound dried penne pasta

1 leek (white part plus 1 inch of green), well washed and thinly sliced crosswise (about 1 cup)

1 bunch spinach, well washed, tough stems removed, coarsely chopped (about 2 cups)

1 cup finely grated fontina

¾ cup finely grated Parmigiano-Reggiano

½ cup heavy cream

1. Preheat the oven to 375°F. Butter a shallow, 12-inch-square baking dish and set it aside.

2. Pour 6 quarts water into a large, heavy-bottomed pot and bring the water to a boil over high heat. Add 2 tablespoons salt.

3. While waiting for the water to boil, melt the 4 tablespoons butter in a pan over medium heat. When the butter becomes a light nut brown, add the sage and poppy seeds, remove the pan from the heat, and set aside.

4. When the water has boiled, add the pasta. When the water returns to a boil, begin to time the pasta carefully; after 8 minutes, add the leek. After

the water has again returned to a boil, add the spinach and cook for an additional 2 minutes. Drain the pasta and vegetables in a colander, return them to the hot pot, add the sage butter, 1 teaspoon salt, 1 teaspoon pepper, the fontina, Parmigiano-Reggiano, and cream and toss well to incorporate the ingredients.

5.   Turn the pasta out into the greased baking dish. Bake for 12 to 15 minutes, until the cheese has melted and the top edges begin to brown.

6.   Serve family style from the center of the table.

YOUR NIGHTLY SPECIALS

BAKED PASTA PRIMAVERA: To create a baked pasta primavera—an excellent side dish to roasted meats and fish—use half as much pasta and a total of 3 to 4 cups blanched, chopped spinach, leeks, broccoli, mushrooms, zucchini, and/or carrots. Use Gruyère cheese to allow the dish to be paired successfully with as many dishes as possible. (Blue and fontina cheeses are too assertive for this recipe and Parmesan alone won't make enough of an impact.)

ONE OR MORE OF THE FOLLOWING cheeses would be delicious in place of those in the recipe: mozzarella, Taleggio and/or Gruyère.

OTHER LARGE PASTA SHAPES such as rigatoni, farfalle (bow ties), or orecchiette (ear shaped) also work well.

FOR A SUBTLE DIFFERENCE, replace the leeks and spinach with zucchini, cut into matchsticks and blanched. Finish with some chopped fresh tomato, whose acidity will fill in for the leek's earthy onion flavor.

USE BLANCHED SWISS CHARD leaves for the spinach or in addition to it to add a richer vegetal flavor.

FRESH OR DRIED BASIL and parsley are perfect substitutes for the sage and poppy seeds.

SPAGHETTI WITH SEASONAL PESTO

SERVES 6 TO 8 AS AN APPETIZER OR 4 AS A MAIN COURSE

How does pesto lend itself to a nightly special? Let me count the ways: it can be stored in the refrigerator or freezer. It's easy to make, so it can be whipped up at the last minute from just a handful of ingredients. And there are endless ways to use it, from tossing it with pasta as here, to topping a pasta salad, to topping a pizza, to providing a depth of flavor to any number of soups.

Pesto is traditionally made with oil and basil, crushed with garlic, pine nuts, and cheese in a mortar and pestle, but now there are so many versions of it that you're likely to see the classic called basil pesto, even though, technically speaking, the name is redundant. Here are two pestos: a classic that you can make in the summer when fresh, fragrant basil is abundant, and a wintertime version using parsley and walnuts in place of basil and pine nuts.

Fine sea salt

1 pound spaghetti

3 tablespoons extra virgin olive oil

½ cup homemade basil or parsley pesto (recipe follows)

Grated Parmigiano-Reggiano

1. Pour 6 quarts water into a large, heavy-bottomed pot and bring the water to a boil over high heat. Add 2 tablespoons salt. Add the spaghetti and cook until al dente, about 8 minutes.

2. Meanwhile, warm a wide, heavy-bottomed sauté pan over medium heat for a minute or two. Pour in the oil, add the pesto, and cook for 1 minute, stirring.

3. Reserve 1 cup of the pasta's cooking liquid, then drain the pasta and add it to the pan with the pesto. Toss for 1 minute, adding small amounts of pasta water to moisten and bind the sauce. (You need not use all of the water.)

4. Divide the spaghetti among individual plates, top with grated cheese, and serve.

BASIL PESTO

MAKES ABOUT 1½ CUPS

MAKE A VINAIGRETTE by whisking 2 tablespoons pesto with 2 tablespoons red wine vinegar, then emulsifying with ½ cup olive oil. Spoon over sliced tomatoes for a quick salad.

THIN THE PESTO with more oil and use it as a dressing for grilled chicken, fish, and/or vegetables.

USE CILANTRO in place of basil, omitting the nuts, and adding a few tablespoons chopped chiles.

2 cups basil leaves (parsley may be substituted)

½ cup extra virgin olive oil

4 garlic cloves, or more to taste, smashed

¼ cup pine nuts (if making with parsley, walnuts may be substituted)

Fine sea salt and freshly ground black pepper

¼ cup grated Parmigiano-Reggiano

1. Put the basil in the bowl of a food processor fitted with the metal blade and process to chop. With the motor running, add half the oil in a thin stream, then add the garlic, nuts, 1 teaspoon salt, and 1 teaspoon pepper. Pulse for another 30 seconds, then scrape down the sides and pulse again. Add the cheese and pulse for 10 seconds.

2. Divide the pesto among small containers and top off each one with some of the remaining oil to keep the pesto from turning brown. The pesto will keep, refrigerated, for up to 1 month, or frozen for up to 6 months.

LINGUINE WITH MANILA CLAMS AND SPICY SAUSAGE

SERVES 6 AS AN APPETIZER OR 4 AS A MAIN COURSE

I WOULDN'T SAY that anything goes in the kitchen, but I am an ardent supporter of improvisation. This recipe respects Italian tradition but uses ingredients from around the world in a way that makes it unique, combining the spiciness of paprika-tinged chorizo sausage and the brininess of shellfish. Clams have a distinct flavor of their own, but get along well with other foods, absorbing the qualities of whatever they're cooked with. Here, they take on the spices and richness of the chorizo.

Fine sea salt and freshly ground black pepper

¼ cup olive oil

3 or 4 olive oil–packed flat anchovy fillets, drained, rinsed, patted dry, and roughly chopped, optional

½ cup onion cut into small dice

½ pound cured chorizo (see page 96) or other lightly spicy, Spanish-style sausage, sliced into ¼-inch rounds

2 dozen fresh Manila clams, in their shells, well scrubbed

2 tablespoons chopped garlic

One 15.5-ounce can plum tomatoes, seeded and crushed, with their juice

½ cup dry white wine

1 pound dried linguine or spaghetti

¼ cup basil leaves cut into julienne

½ cup chopped flat-leaf parsley

1. Bring 6 quarts water to a boil in a large, heavy-bottomed pot over high heat; add 2 tablespoons salt.

2. While the water is coming to a boil, heat the oil in a saucepan over medium heat. Add the chopped anchovy fillets, if using, and sauté over medium heat until the anchovies begin to melt and dissolve, about 2 minutes. Add the onion and chorizo and sauté until the chorizo begins to brown, about 5 minutes. Add the clams and the garlic. When the garlic has softened but not browned, add the tomatoes, season with salt and pepper,

REPLACE THE CHORIZO with Italian-style fresh hot sausage, or skip the sausage entirely and use tiny shrimp called brine shrimp. If you leave out the chorizo and don't replace it with any other sausage, you'll have a good, basic red clam sauce to which you can add mussels and/or diced and sautéed red and green bell peppers.

SPICE UP THE SAUCE with a last-second addition of cayenne or crushed red pepper flakes.

SKIP THE PASTA and serve the sauce over steamed rice.

and cook until the tomatoes begin to break down, 5 minutes. Pour in the white wine, cover the pan, and cook until the clams steam open, about 5 minutes.

3. Meanwhile, add the pasta to the boiling water and cook until al dente, about 9 minutes. Drain the pasta and transfer it to a large serving bowl.

4. When the clams are done, use tongs to remove and discard any that have not opened. Add the basil to the pan with the sauce and continue cooking for just a minute. Remove the pan from the heat.

5. Mound some pasta on each plate and spoon some sauce over the pasta, being sure to include some chorizo and clams in each serving. Top each portion with parsley and serve at once.

Chorizo

Its name is used by many as a generic way to reference spicy sausage from Spain and Latin America, but in reality there are dozens of types of chorizo. It's available in fresh, partly cured, and dried forms.

COCONUT-SCENTED BASMATI RICE

SERVES 4 TO 6 AS A SIDE DISH

BASMATI RICE IS THE CENTERPIECE of Indian and Pakistani cooking. I'm fascinated by how the individual grains elongate rather than plump as they cook, helping them keep their firm-textured shape without breaking down. Basmati's sweet, almost perfumed, floral aroma also makes it very appealing as a simple, steamed rice.

2 tablespoons olive oil

1 small onion, minced (about ½ cup)

2 cups basmati rice, or other similar long-grained rice, picked over for stones and rinsed of excess starch

1 bay leaf

Fine sea salt

3 cups homemade chicken stock (page 69), low-sodium, store-brought chicken broth, vegetable broth, or water, simmering in a pot set over medium heat

Freshly ground white pepper

5 tablespoons unsalted butter

½ cup unsweetened coconut milk

¼ cup chopped cilantro

YOUR NIGHTLY SPECIALS

ADD TOASTED COCONUT, raisins plumped in hot water, and/or crushed almonds or walnuts during the last few minutes of cooking.

ADD ⅛ TEASPOON CAYENNE pepper while the rice is cooking.

ADD A PEELED, JULIENNED LARGE CARROT while the rice is cooking.

FOR SAFFRON RICE, add a pinch of saffron threads to the broth.

1.   Heat the oil in a large, heavy-bottomed pot over medium heat. Add the onion and sauté until softened but not browned, about 4 minutes. Add the rice and stir to coat well with the oil, then add the bay leaf, 1 teaspoon salt, and hot broth. Season lightly with pepper. Bring to a boil over high heat, cover the pot with a tight-fitting lid, reduce the heat, and let simmer, removing the lid occasionally to stir with a fork to prevent scorching, until the grains are fully cooked but not clumped together, 18 to 20 minutes.

2.   Use tongs to remove and discard the bay leaf. Use a fork to gently stir and separate the grains and stir in the butter, coconut milk, and cilantro.

3.   Transfer the rice to a serving dish, or spoon it alongside other components, and serve at once.

PAELLA WITH CHICKEN AND SAUSAGE

SERVES 4

Some dishes are an event in themselves. Paella is one such classic, in part because of its riot of bright colors—yellow Valencia rice, burnt-orange saffron, green peas, and red sausage. Like risotto, paella requires its own rice. Valencia is traditional, but any Spanish rice that's medium-grained and not too starchy will do. Look for it in the Latin American or international foods section of the supermarket.

While a two-handled paella pan is traditional, it is not necessary to buy one for this dish. A three- or four-quart heatproof, ovenproof casserole or Dutch oven–type pot will work just as well. If necessary, you can also brown the meat in a pan, then transfer it to a separate ovenproof casserole.

¼ cup olive oil

2 pounds chicken meat, dark and light, on the bone with the skin intact, cut through the bone into smaller segments of breast and thigh meat

Fine sea salt and freshly ground black pepper

1 pound fresh, Spanish-style chorizo sausage, cut crosswise into coin-size rounds

1 onion, diced (about ½ cup)

¼ teaspoon saffron threads, soaked in ¼ cup hot water for 10 minutes

1 cup Valencia or other Spanish rice, picked over

2½ cups homemade chicken stock (page 69) or low-sodium, store-bought chicken broth

½ cup fresh green peas or defrosted frozen peas

1. Preheat the oven to 350°F.

2. Set the paella pan over medium heat. Pour in 2 tablespoons of the oil and let it get nice and hot. Season the chicken with salt and pepper, add it to the pan, and brown it all over, about 8 minutes. Transfer the chicken to a platter and set aside.

3. Add the remaining 2 tablespoons oil to the pan. Add the sausage slices to the pan and brown them for 3 to 4 minutes. Add the onion and cook until softened, about 4 minutes.

NIGHTLY SPECIALS

ADD PEELED, DEVEINED SHRIMP, cubed monkfish tail, or steamed, chopped lobster meat to the pan with the chicken; just make sure you use a pan or casserole large enough to hold all the ingredients.

ADD SHELLFISH such as clams and/or mussels after the initial browning of the chicken.

4. Return the chicken to the pan. Add the soaked saffron threads with their liquid, the rice, and broth, stir, and bring to a boil over high heat. Lower the heat and let simmer over low heat for 5 minutes. Transfer the pan to the oven and bake for 20 minutes.

5. Remove the pan from the oven. Stir in the peas, return the pan to the oven, and cook for 2 more minutes.

6. Serve the paella from its pan or a festive serving dish or bowl. Present it with a large spoon so people can take the heaps they'll want.

JAMBALAYA WITH SHRIMP AND CHICKEN

SERVES 4 TO 6 AS A MAIN COURSE

RISOTTO MIGHT REMIND US OF ITALY, *paella reminds us of Spain, and jambalaya belongs not to one country but is the property of one state: Louisiana.* No matter who you are or where you live, jambalaya transports you to New Orleans, with its intensely flavored Cajun cuisine. Many Louisiana dishes vary from restaurant to restaurant, just as jazz standards are reinterpreted by individual musicians. This is my jambalaya, and I hope you'll use it as a guideline to make your own version, perhaps adding more shrimp or sausage, or varying the herbs. In the spirit of New Orleans, I never make mine the same way twice.

3 tablespoons olive oil

1 pound boneless, skinless chicken breast, cut into ¼-inch-thick strips

1 pound andouille sausage or smoked sausage, cut into coin-shaped rounds

1 large onion, cut into medium dice

1 large green or red pepper, stemmed and seeded and cut into medium dice

1 celery stalk, cut into medium dice

2 tablespoons chopped garlic

1 tablespoon chopped thyme

½ teaspoon cayenne pepper

1 teaspoon oregano

1 cup crushed canned tomatoes, with their juice

2 bay leaves

½ cup diced tasso ham (Cajun spiced, country, or Virginia ham can be substituted)

2 cups long-grain white rice

Fine sea salt and freshly ground black pepper

1 pound medium shrimp, peeled and deveined

1 cup scallions cut into small dice

1. Heat the oil in a large, heavy-bottomed pot over medium-high heat. Add the chicken and brown it all over, about 8 minutes. Remove the chicken to a plate and set aside.

2. Add the sausage to the pot and brown it well, about 6 minutes. Add the onion, pepper, and celery and cook until wilted, about 10 minutes. Add the garlic, thyme, cayenne, oregano, tomatoes, bay leaves, and tasso.

NIGHTLY SPECIALS

OMIT THE CHICKEN and make an all-seafood jambalaya: stir in scallops and firm fish fillets (black bass, snapper, or redfish would be ideal) cut into 1-inch cubes along with the shrimp.

ADD SOME ROASTED FRESH PORK loin to the sausage and chicken and leave out the shrimp.

USE KIELBASA in place of the andouille sausage.

ADD VEGETABLES: diced mirliton or chayote would be very authentic. Sautéed, diced eggplant and zucchini would also work. For a vegetarian version, leave out the chicken, sausage, and shrimp and use all of these vegetables.

3. Return the chicken to the pot, add the rice, stir well, and cook for 2 to 3 minutes over medium heat. Pour in 4 cups water, season with salt and pepper, and raise the heat to high to bring to a boil. Lower the heat until the liquid is simmering, partially cover, and let simmer for 20 minutes. Stir in the shrimp and cook for another 5 minutes. Stir in the scallions.

4. Spoon heaping portions into wide, shallow bowls and serve.

RISOTTO

SERVES 6 TO 8 AS AN APPETIZER OR 4 AS A MAIN COURSE

Risotto is one of the most versatile dishes to have in your bag of culinary tricks. Once you master the basic technique, you can make any risotto you like. The key to making risotto is selecting an appropriate short-grained rice such as Arborio, Canaroli, or Vialone Nano and patiently adding broth or stock, stirring until each addition is absorbed before adding the next. This process gradually releases the rice's starch, which is the element that binds risotto grains together. I keep some risotto rice on hand at all times, knowing that if the pantry is bare I can whip up a risotto with fresh vegetables and shellfish.

3 tablespoons olive oil

1 large onion, cut into small dice

2 cups Arborio rice (or another short-grained variety, such as Canaroli or Vialone Nano)

1 cup dry white wine

5 cups homemade chicken stock (page 69), or low-sodium, store-bought chicken broth simmering in a pot

4 tablespoons (½ stick) unsalted butter

¼ cup grated Parmigiano-Reggiano

¼ cup heavy cream

1. Heat the oil in a wide, deep-sided, heavy-bottomed sauté pan over medium-high heat. Add the onion and sauté until softened but not browned, about 4 minutes.

2. Add the rice, stir to coat it with the oil, and sauté to toast each grain. (This toasting process adds the chewy, al dente quality that attracts so many people to risotto.)

3. Once the rice is lightly toasted, pour in the white wine slowly, stirring with a wooden spoon. (A wooden spoon is always preferable when making risotto, as metal can cut or injure the grains of rice.)

4. After the rice has absorbed the white wine and is nearly dry, add one cup of hot broth, stirring occasionally, and cook over very low heat until

NIGHTLY SPECIALS

YOUR

TO VARY THE RISOTTO:

- stir fresh herbs in at the end

- add sautéed vegetables such as half-moon-shaped slices of zucchini sautéed in olive oil

- sauté shrimp and add them at the last second

- make a take-off on the classic broccoli raab and sausage, sauté crumbled sausage and broccoli raab florets and fold them in at the end

- finish the risotto with chopped flat-leaf parsley and lemon zest

ONE OF THE MOST CANNY VARIATIONS is using red wine, or beet juice, instead of white wine and serving the risotto with roasted meat.

the broth is absorbed by the rice. Continue adding the broth, a cupful at a time, until all of the broth has been absorbed. Adding the liquid in stages, instead of all at once, allows the rice grains to expand more fully, adding to risotto's creamy texture. Once the rice has been added to the pan, this process will take 17 to 20 minutes;

5. After all the liquid has been added, and the rice is chewy yet fully cooked, with a creamy texture, add the butter, cheese, and cream. Stir to combine and serve immediately.

SUPERMARKET MUSHROOM RISOTTO

SERVES 6 TO 8 AS AN APPETIZER OR 4 AS A MAIN COURSE

MUSHROOM RISOTTO is one of the most popular versions of this rice dish, often used as a vehicle for wild mushrooms like chanterelles. This recipe will show you that if you take the time to carefully season and cook all of your ingredients, even plain button mushrooms can offer unforgettable flavor. Here, the mushrooms are sautéed with butter, shallots, garlic, thyme, and cream, making them truly sublime when folded into the risotto.

2 tablespoons unsalted butter

2 tablespoons minced shallots

1 garlic clove, minced

One 10-ounce package white button mushrooms, ends trimmed, sliced as thinly as possible

2 tablespoons chopped thyme

3 tablespoons heavy cream

Fine sea salt and freshly ground black pepper

Risotto (page 102)

¼ cup grated Parmigiano-Reggiano

YOUR NIGHTLY SPECIALS

USE AS MANY MUSHROOMS AS YOU LIKE, such as chanterelle, oyster, hen of the woods, and black trumpet. Sauté each one on its own because they all cook at different rates.

USE SAGE for a powerful, autumnal alternative to thyme.

1.   Melt the butter in a sauté pan over medium-high heat. Add the shallots and garlic and sauté until softened but not browned, about 4 minutes. Add the mushrooms and cook, stirring gently, until softened and they begin to release their liquid, about 6 minutes. Stir in the thyme and cream and season with salt and pepper.

2.   Stir the mushrooms into the risotto. Divide among individual plates or bowls and top with grated cheese and a few grinds of black pepper.

QUINOA "RISOTTO" WITH TOASTED HAZELNUTS AND DRIED CURRANTS

SERVES 4 TO 6 AS A SIDE DISH

ONCE THE STAPLE FOOD of the great Inca civilization, quinoa is actually a plant but acts like a grain in cooking. It's full-flavored, with a slightly bitter taste, and has been used for beer, soups, and stews for millennia. It's a nutritionally complex food and superior in many ways to other grains. This dish, in which the quinoa is cooked like a risotto with successive additions of stock, was a nightly special at a time when I first became interested in Latin American cooking and discovered quinoa in some Ecuadorian recipes.

½ cup hazelnuts

1 tablespoon olive oil

1 small onion, cut into small dice

1 cup quinoa, washed in cold running water and drained

2 cups homemade chicken stock (page 69) or low-sodium, store-bought chicken broth

1 bay leaf

1 tablespoon ground cinnamon

½ cup dried currants, dried cranberries, or raisins

Fine sea salt and freshly ground black pepper

2 tablespoons unsalted butter

1. Toast the hazelnuts in a heavy-bottomed sauté pan over medium heat, shaking the pan, until they become warm and fragrant, about 4 minutes. Remove the pan from the heat and gently rub the hazelnuts in a kitchen towel to remove the skins. Chop coarsely and set aside.

2. Heat the oil in a small saucepan over medium-high heat for 1 minute. Add the onion and sauté until softened but not browned, about 4 minutes. Stir in the quinoa and toast the grains for 1 minute. Pour in half the broth and bring it to a boil over high heat. Lower the heat so the liquid is simmering, add the bay leaf, cinnamon, currants, ½ teaspoon salt and ½ teaspoon pepper and cook until all the liquid is absorbed, about 8 minutes. Add the remaining broth, bring to a boil, then lower the heat and simmer another 8 minutes.

NIGHTLY SPECIALS

USE TOASTED, CHOPPED WALNUTS or almonds instead of hazelnuts.

ADD DRIED, DICED APRICOTS and dates, diced raw McIntosh apple, and/or pumpkin spices along with the nuts and butter.

3. Stir in the nuts and butter, remove the pan from the heat, cover the pan, and let sit for 5 minutes. Taste and correct the seasoning with salt and pepper.

4. Transfer the quinoa to a serving bowl and serve.

CURRIED WHEAT BERRIES WITH SWEET ONIONS

SERVES 4 AS A SIDE DISH

WHEAT BERRIES—the whole, unprocessed kernel of wheat— are widely available but not very familiar to most cooks. Cooked as they are here, they are pleasingly crunchy and nutty. Use them as an accompaniment to roasted game or game birds or as an addition to your holiday table. Their richly flavored, unprocessed quality make them a vehicle for carrying the flavors of Turkish lamb or other full-flavored dishes.

1 cup wheat berries

Fine sea salt and freshly ground black pepper

4 tablespoons unsalted butter

1 large onion, cut into small dice

4 tablespoons curry powder

2 whole star anise

1. Put the wheat berry kernels in a bowl and cover with 2 cups cold water. Soak them overnight. (This will increase their volume threefold and make them easier to cook.)

2. Drain the berries and put them in a lidded pot. Pour in 5 cups water. Add 1 teaspoon salt and ½ teaspoon pepper. Cover and bring to a boil over high heat. Reduce the heat and simmer until the berries are tender but still retain some crunch, 1 hour to 1 hour and 15 minutes. Drain any excess liquid.

3. While the wheat berries cook, melt 2 tablespoons of the butter in a sauté pan over medium heat. Add the onion and sauté until softened but not browned, about 4 minutes. Add the curry powder and star anise pods and cook over low heat, stirring, to toast the curry powder and coat the onion evenly, 1 to 2 minutes. Add the wheat berries and stir to combine

USE BULGUR WHEAT, which is cracked and cooks more quickly, or use pearl barley, also a nutty and tasty alternative to potatoes.

INSTEAD OF BUTTER, begin step 3 with diced slab bacon and add the next ingredients after the bacon has rendered enough fat to coat the bottom of the pan.

ADD DICED CARROTS, chopped almonds, and/or chopped pecans to the berries halfway through the cooking time.

well. Pour in ¼ cup water. Cover the sauté pan and cook over medium heat for 10 minutes. Stir in the remaining 2 tablespoons butter and adjust the seasoning with salt and pepper.

4. Transfer the berries to a serving bowl and serve immediately.

TOASTED BARLEY AND BUTTERNUT SQUASH

SERVES 4

THIS SPECIAL WAS SERVED at the annual Thanksgiving dinner at Windows on the World. Barley isn't often seen outside the soup pot, but it's so rich and rewarding that there's every reason to serve it with sweet, autumnal vegetables like squash. Add spices and cinnamon and maple syrup and my pilgrim fantasy is complete.

2 tablespoons unsalted butter

1 small onion, minced

1 cup pearl barley or coarse-grained hulled barley, picked over, rinsed, and drained

2 cups homemade chicken stock (page 69) or low-sodium, store-bought chicken broth, simmering in a pot

1 medium butternut squash (about 1½ pounds), peeled, halved lengthwise, seeded, and cut into 1-inch cubes

2 tablespoons olive oil

Fine sea salt and freshly ground black pepper

3 tablespoons maple syrup

1 teaspoon ground cinnamon

¼ teaspoon ground cloves

¼ teaspoon freshly ground nutmeg

Fresh sage leaves, for garnish

1. Preheat the oven to 375°F.

2. Melt the butter in a large, heavy-bottomed pot over medium-high heat. Add the onion and cook until softened and lightly golden, about 6 minutes. Add the barley, stir, and cook for 3 minutes, continuing to stir to prevent the barley from scorching.

3. Pour in the hot broth, stir, and cook uncovered at a simmer until the broth is absorbed and the barley is tender but still a bit al dente, about 40 minutes.

4. Meanwhile, put the squash and oil in a bowl and toss. Season with salt and pepper, toss again, turn out onto a cookie sheet in a single layer, and

USE OTHER WINTER SQUASH like Hubbard or small pumpkins instead of butternut.

ADD SOME DICED, SMOKED HAM along with the onion in step 2.

DRIZZLE SOME MOLASSES over the finished dish and/or top the serving bowl with thinly sliced ripe pears.

roast the squash in the oven until tender, 15 to 20 minutes, when pierced with a sharp, thin-bladed knife. Add the syrup, cinnamon, cloves, and nutmeg, stir, and roast for another 10 minutes.

5. Stir the roasted squash into the barley. Transfer to a serving dish, top with sage leaves, and serve.

SOFT HERBED POLENTA

SERVES 4 AS A SIDE DISH

EVEN THOUGH I GREW UP in an Italian-American home, polenta, the northern Italian staple, wasn't served. But it quickly became a nightly special when I was a sous chef at '21' working under chefs Alain Sailhac and Anne Rosensweig and they let me create the lunch specials. I introduced soft polenta, new at the time to the staid, buttoned-down crowd, and it eventually became so popular that it was given a permanent place on the menu as an accompaniment to venison chops.

2 cups milk

1 cup cold water

Fine sea salt

1 cup yellow cornmeal

4 tablespoons (½ stick) unsalted butter

3 tablespoons finely grated Parmigiano-Reggiano

3 tablespoons chopped fresh herbs, such as thyme, parsley, and/or chives

NIGHTLY SPECIALS

USE CRUMBLED BLUE CHEESE instead of the Parmigiano-Reggiano.

STIR IN CHOPPED SAGE just before serving.

ADD ½ CUP FRESHLY COOKED CORN kernels at the end.

STIR IN BROWNED CUBES OF SMOKED BACON and caramelized onions.

1.   Pour the milk and water into a heavy-bottomed, 2- or 3-quart pot. Add ½ teaspoon salt and the cornmeal and stir with a whisk to eliminate any lumps. Set over medium-high heat and heat just to a boil, being careful not to scorch the milk or cornmeal. Reduce the heat to very low and let the mixture simmer until the liquid is almost totally absorbed, about 25 minutes, stirring occasionally with a wooden spoon. If, near the end of the cooking, the polenta is becoming too thick and heavy to stir, add 1 or more tablespoons of cold water to loosen the mixture enough to be able to stir it, and to maintain a creamy consistency.

2.   Stir in the butter, incorporating it quickly. (Use more if you like it very buttery.) Stir in the cheese and herbs.

3.   Transfer the polenta to a serving bowl or spoon alongside meat or poultry on a plate.

THE SHELL

Shellfish, Large and Small

GAME

From roasted lobster to pots of steamed mussels, our attraction to sweet, succulent shellfish draws us time and again to restaurants, clam bars, roadside crab shacks, and fish-fry joints from coast to coast. And yet millions of shellfish lovers, even those who cook on a regular basis, shudder at the prospect of preparing these items at home.

The first thing to do is identify a fish market or food shop in your area that sells fresh fish and shellfish. Even in relatively landlocked areas, there is usually at least one market that brings in fresh catches. Yes, shellfish can be costly, but thoughtful menu planning can find a place for them in any budget, even if it means using them as a starter or as part of a larger menu.

Now that you've got a reliable source, always buy the freshest shellfish available, remembering that the market you're buying in must be trustworthy enough to guarantee freshness. Buy all soft-shell crabs, clams, mussels, oysters, and lobster live and in the shell if possible, though you can sometimes purchase just-shucked oysters and flash-frozen soft-shell crabs that are perfectly fine. Crabmeat is sold as a cooked and processed food, and while I prefer fresh-picked crabmeat, sometimes you can find only pasteurized, canned crabmeat, which can be used in sauces, stuffing, or even crab cakes, but shouldn't be used in, say, salads, where the emphasis is on the crab's freshness.

After sorting through shellfish for debris and discarding opened or damaged shells, wash it under cold running water to remove sand. Do not soak clams or oysters in water. Mussels may be soaked for 15 to 18 minutes, but change the water often and shake them so that they stay alive. For oysters and clams that are to be served on the half shell, keep them in their closed shells, on crushed ice, and refrigerated until you intend to shuck them; they open much more readily when well chilled.

Lobster is best when alive and kept in saltwater tanks. Store live lobsters in the colder, lower areas of your refrigerator. Do not leave live lobsters in tightly closed plastic bags; rather, store them loosely packed in wet newspaper, so that the moisture keeps them especially cold.

Shrimp is sold frozen or previously frozen and defrosted, 95 percent of the time. This, too, is acceptable. But at certain times of the year, you'll find fresh shrimp, and those are the times to snatch it up and make it the subject of a special. It costs more, and it's worth every cent.

Squid, also known by its Italian name, calamari, is also sold frozen and fresh and is acceptable in either form for most dishes. If you know it only as something to be breaded and fried, there's a Spanish-style casserole coming up that will open your eyes to its many possibilities.

Judging by what I've seen in my restaurant experience, a lot of you love scallops. Whether they are sautéed, deep-fried, poached in a stew, or marinated raw in a ceviche, we adore these sweet shellfish morsels. Sea scallops are meatier and brinier than tiny bay scallops, and they both have distinct ideal applications: sea scallops are big enough to stand up to the heat of a grill or a hot sauté pan; little bays are best handled with a gentle hand and should not be overpowered in the cooking process. While the scallop is a bivalve—meaning it comes from a shell—we rarely think of it as a raw shellfish choice. That will change after you've made your first ceviche and taken your deserved bows.

MARYLAND-STYLE CRAB CAKES

MAKES 6 TO 8 CRAB CAKES, ENOUGH TO SERVE 4 TO 6 AS AN APPETIZER
OR 4 AS A MAIN COURSE

BECAUSE IT'S HANDPICKED, *fresh crabmeat can be expensive. So this dish is presented as an appetizer to make it as economical as possible, though you could definitely double the recipe and serve it as a main course for four people. "Maryland-style" refers to crabmeat made into patties with a variety of seasonings, especially Old Bay, which gives it that unmistakable Chesapeake Bay flavor. For a light meal, serve this on the same plate with Curly Endive Salad with Warm Bacon Vinaigrette (page 15).*

1 pound fresh jumbo-lump crabmeat, preferably blue crab, picked through for shell fragments (see page 118)

1 red bell pepper, stemmed and seeded and cut into small dice

1 yellow bell pepper, stemmed and seeded and cut into small dice

1 tablespoon minced garlic

1 to 2 jalapeño peppers, seeded and cut into small dice

⅓ cup chopped cilantro

⅓ cup mayonnaise

2 tablespoons Old Bay seasoning

2 cups fresh white breadcrumbs

Fine sea salt and freshly ground black pepper

Olive oil or vegetable oil

Chile Mayonnaise (recipe follows)

1. Stir together gently in a bowl the crabmeat, bell peppers, garlic, jalapeño, cilantro, and mayonnaise. Scatter the Old Bay seasoning, ½ cup of the breadcrumbs, ½ teaspoon salt, and ½ teaspoon pepper over the mixture, then stir gently but thoroughly. Cover the bowl and chill in the refrigerator for 20 minutes (a cold mixture is easier to work with and shape into cakes).

2. Cover a work surface with waxed paper and sprinkle half of the remaining breadcrumbs over it. Scoop up and divide the crabmeat into 4 to 8 equal portions and place each mound on the work surface. Roll 1 portion of crab in the crumbs, put it in the palm of one hand, and pat it with

USE CANNED SALMON, picked through for any bone fragments, or day-old Cold Poached Salmon (page 172).

your other hand into a tight, trim, disc-shaped cake, about 2 inches in diameter and ¾ inch thick. Repeat with the remaining portions, making sure they are the same thickness to ensure that they cook at the same rate.

3. Spread the remaining breadcrumbs out on the work surface and roll the cakes, one at a time, in the crumbs to coat them evenly on all sides. Put the crab cakes in a single layer on 1 or 2 plates, cover loosely with plastic wrap, and refrigerate for at least 1 hour, or overnight, so that they firm up enough to keep them from crumbling when cooked.

4. Pour enough oil into the bottom of a wide, deep-sided, heavy-bottomed sauté pan to cover the surface and heat over medium heat until hot but not smoking. Add the crab cakes gingerly, being careful not to crowd the pan. (You might need to cook the crab cakes in two batches.) Brown one side, about 3 minutes, then carefully turn the cakes over with a spatula and brown them on the other side, another 2 to 3 minutes. If browning the cakes in batches, transfer the cooked cakes to a nonstick cookie sheet and keep in a warm oven; add some more oil to the pan and let it heat up before browning the second batch.

5. Divide the crab cakes among 4 to 8 plates and drizzle some chile mayonnaise decoratively over each serving. Serve at once.

Working with crabmeat

Even though crabmeat is packaged fresh and is marketed as having been cleaned of shell, there are always some shell fragments remaining. Open the crabmeat, turn it out onto a clean dish, and with scrupulously clean hands, pick through and clean the crabmeat of all shell fragments. When working with lump crabmeat, respect its delicate nature by taking care not to crumble the large pieces. This caution will reward you with a rich texture in whatever dish you're making.

CHILE MAYONNAISE
MAKES ABOUT 1¼ CUPS MAYONNAISE

2 ounces whole, dried ancho, chipotle, cascabel, New Mexico, or other chiles or 2 tablespoons ancho chile powder

1 cup homemade or store-bought mayonnaise

If using whole chiles, stem and seed them and put them in a bowl. Pour enough boiling water over the chiles to cover them and let soak for 30 minutes. Drain the chiles, reserving their soaking liquid, and puree them thoroughly in a blender, adding some soaking liquid to help liquefy them. If using chile powder, put the powder in a bowl and add ¼ cup boiling water. Stir and let cool. (This paste can be covered and refrigerated for up to 10 days or, if covered with a thin film of oil, several weeks.) Put the paste and mayonnaise in a bowl and stir them together. This mayonnaise can be covered and refrigerated for up to 1 week.

GRILLED SOFT-SHELL CRABS WITH LIME, RUM, AND MANGO

SERVES 4

Soft-shell crabs—eastern blue crabs caught within hours of molting their old, hard shell—show up as a nightly special in restaurants from coast to coast every spring. It's impossible to know exactly when they'll appear each year, and when they do, chefs can't wait to get them on the menu. It's the same for many home cooks: you're walking through the market, all of a sudden you see live soft-shell crabs, and you can't believe it's already been twelve months since the last time this happened.

When that moment occurs next year, scrap your plans for dinner and buy some soft-shell crabs and the rest of the ingredients on this recipe's short list. If you don't live on the east coast, look for soft-shell crabs that are sold cleaned and flash frozen, a good way to satisfy a craving for this much-loved crustacean.

3 tablespoons olive oil

1 jalapeño pepper, seeded and minced

½ red bell pepper, stemmed and seeded, cut into small dice

½ cup grated coconut, preferably fresh

2 tablespoons wildflower honey, at room temperature

Juice of 2 limes (about ¼ cup)

¼ cup light rum

8 fresh, live soft-shell crabs, cleaned (see opposite page)

Fine sea salt and freshly ground black pepper

2 mangos, peeled and sliced into ¼-inch-thick slices

1 bunch watercress, stems discarded, coarsely chopped

2 tablespoons chile oil

1. Stir the olive oil, jalapeño, bell pepper, coconut, honey, lime juice, and rum together in a bowl. Arrange the crabs in a single layer in a shallow baking dish or two, drizzle the olive oil over them, toss gently, cover, and let marinate in the refrigerator for 1 to 2 hours.

2. Prepare an outdoor grill for grilling.

SOFT-SHELL CRAB SANDWICH WITH CHILE MAYONNAISE: This open-faced sandwich is a simple way to enjoy soft-shell crabs without any forethought or planning: dredge 4 crabs in 1 cup all-purpose flour, then 1 cup milk, then 1 cup cornmeal. Season the crabs with salt and pepper. Heat some vegetable oil in a cast-iron skillet and fry the crabs until crisp, about 3 minutes per side. Arrange 2 slices of Pullman bread on each of 4 plates. Top each slice with lettuce, tomato, and a crab. Drizzle some Chile Mayonnaise (page 119) over each crab and serve.

3. Remove the crabs from the marinade, letting any excess marinade run off. Season them with salt and pepper. Cook the crabs on the grill, making sure that they are not directly over the flame, and basting with the remaining marinade, until the shells brown and crisp, 2 to 3 minutes per side. The smaller the crabs, the more quickly they cook; larger ones can take up to 4 minutes per side.

4. Fan some mango slices in the center of each of 4 plates. Top each mango fan with 2 crabs and arrange the watercress decoratively around them. Drizzle with chile oil and serve.

Cleaning soft-shell crabs

The easiest way to clean soft-shell crabs is to have your fishmonger do it for you, bring them home, and cook them as soon as possible on the same day. It is, however, useful to know how to clean soft-shell crabs, and here's how:

Rinse the crab under cold running water. Snip off the mouth parts (front pincers and eyes), which will kill them instantly. Remove the gills, apron, and front pincers: the gills are located under each winglike side of the shell; lift the top shell and you'll find the feathery, tendril-like gills on the body surface underneath. Use your fingertips to pull away and discard them. The apron—which, yes, looks like an apron—is found on the crab's underside, concealing its rear half. It, too, lifts up and should be cut away with scissors.

ROASTED OYSTERS WITH COUNTRY BACON

THIS RECIPE is a take on the famous pan roast that's been served at the Oyster Bar on the lower level of New York City's Grand Central Station for decades. Many oyster lovers prefer them on the half shell, but lightly poaching them coaxes out their briny, refreshing character for a sublime, full-flavored taste.

24 fresh oysters, purchased in their shells, shucked, shells reserved (see opposite page)

¼ pound sliced bacon

2 cups loosely packed spinach leaves

Fine sea salt and freshly ground black pepper

3 tablespoons unsalted butter

3 large shallots, minced (about ¼ cup)

1 teaspoon hot Spanish paprika (preferably smoked paprika)

½ cup dry white wine

1 cup heavy cream

2 plum tomatoes, peeled, seeded, and diced

2 tablespoons chopped flat-leaf parsley

1 tablespoon chopped tarragon, plus more for serving

1. Preheat the oven to 325°F. Put the cleaned oyster shells on a cookie sheet in a single layer and set aside.

2. Heat a heavy-bottomed sauté pan over low heat. Put in the bacon and sauté until crispy and the fat is rendered, about 8 minutes. Transfer the bacon to a paper towel-lined plate to drain, then roughly chop it and set aside.

3. Pour off and discard all but 2 tablespoons of the bacon fat and put the pan over medium-high heat. Add the spinach, season with salt, and sauté it quickly, just until the leaves are wilted, about 30 seconds. Transfer some spinach to each oyster shell and pack it down gently.

4. Put the cookie sheet with the filled oyster shells in the oven.

5. Add the butter to the same sauté pan and melt it over medium-high heat just until it begins to foam. Add the shallots and paprika and cook,

INSTEAD OF WINE, use dry sherry or port for richer flavor.

LEAVE OUT THE BACON, skip step 2, and begin step 3 by heating 2 tablespoons olive oil in the pan.

ADD DICED, SAUTÉED FENNEL and, if desired, a splash of anise-flavored liqueur like Pernod, along with the spinach.

LEAVE OUT THE TOMATOES.

DON'T USE SPINACH OR OYSTER SHELLS: instead, serve the oysters and sauce over toasted, buttered brioche.

ONE OF MY FAVORITE DISHES in the world is made by cooking this recipe with extra bacon, leaving out the tomatoes, and using dry sherry instead of white wine. Serve this version with lots of crusty bread for dipping or you might be tempted to lick the shells clean.

stirring, for 2 minutes. Add the oysters and their juice and the white wine and sauté for 2 minutes, then pour in the cream. Bring to a quick boil, then reduce the heat and let simmer for just a minute, or until the oysters' edges begin to curl. Add the tomatoes, parsley, tarragon, and bacon and season with pepper. Heat for another 30 seconds, then immediately remove the pan from the heat.

6.   Remove the cookie sheet from the oven and use tongs to arrange 6 filled shells on each of 4 plates. Spoon an oyster onto the spinach in each shell and spoon a little of the sauce over it. Sprinkle additional tarragon over each serving.

To shuck an oyster

Oysters often can be purchased shucked from a fish store, which is fine, so long as they are stored in their liquid. This dish, however, calls for oyster shells, so you'll need to shuck them yourself. (If you purchase your oysters shucked, build the dish in a wide, shallow soup plate.)

Using a towel, grasp an oyster in the palm of your hand. Press the oyster, rounded side down, on a firm surface, still holding it with the towel. Shuck the oyster by wedging the tip of an oyster knife (regular knives are too thin bladed) between the halves of the shell, at the narrow end. When the knife tip is securely wedged, rotate your wrist and the blade to pry open the shell. Slide the knife blade along the length of the shell to open it completely. Remove the oyster from the shell and reserve it, along with its juice.

If the recipe you're preparing calls for shells, from each pair of oyster shells save the one that is more concave on the inside, and discard the flatter one. Put the concave shells in a pan of cold water, scrub them inside and out, rinse, and let dry.

To peel tomatoes

Bring a large pot of water to a boil. Fill a large bowl halfway with ice water. Score the ends of the tomatoes, cut out the stem ends, and put them in the boiling water. After 20 seconds, use tongs to remove the tamatoes from the water and transfer them to the ice water. As they cool, the skin will begin to pull away from the flesh. Remove the tomatoes and peel them with a paring knife.

FRIED OYSTERS WITH MUSTARD TARTAR SAUCE

SERVES 4 TO 6 AS AN APPETIZER

THE PRE-DINNER COCKTAIL HOUR is often the time that home cooks fill bowls with peanuts, pretzels, and/or breadsticks and call it a day. But making wine-and-cocktail-friendly food can be a quick and satisfying way to expand your repertoire. These fried oysters are a real crowd pleaser, and the tartar dipping sauce—based on the classic French remoulade—really puts them over the top. I don't often make drink suggestions, but do yourself a favor and savor these with an ice-cold beer or a glass of champagne.

1½ cups all-purpose flour, plus more for dredging

1 tablespoon baking soda

Fine sea salt

¼ teaspoon cayenne pepper

1 teaspoon chili powder

1 egg

¾ cup buttermilk

About 1 cup canola oil, for frying

12 oysters, shucked (see page 123)

Mustard Tartar Sauce (recipe follows)

1. Put the flour, baking soda, ½ teaspoon salt, cayenne pepper, and chili powder in a bowl. Whisk in the egg, buttermilk, and ½ cup water, taking care not to make the batter too smooth and homogenized. Cover the bowl with plastic wrap and let the batter rest in the refrigerator for 30 minutes, or up to 2 hours. (This is a good time to make the Mustard Tartar Sauce if you haven't already.)

2. Heat about ½ cup oil in a deep, heavy-bottomed sauté pan over high heat. Put some flour on a plate, dredge the oysters in the flour one at a time, then dip each oyster into the batter and immediately place in the hot oil. Fry the oysters 6 to 8 at a time until they begin to crisp on the surface and turn golden brown, about 2 minutes. Turn them over and fry the other

side, about 2 more minutes. As they are done, set them on a paper towel–lined plate to drain. Replace the oil with clean, fresh oil and cook the rest of the oysters in batches.

3. Serve the oysters from a serving platter with the tartar sauce alongside.

INSTEAD OF OYSTERS, bread and fry the largest mussels you can find. First, steam them open with ¼ cup white wine for about 3 minutes, then let them cool. Discard any that have not opened, shell them, cool, and proceed with the oyster recipe.

USE CHILE MAYONNAISE (page 119) or make wasabi mayonnaise by stirring a few tablespoons of wasabi paste into mayonnaise.

IF IT'S EASIER FOR YOU, make these with the classic coating of all-purpose flour, beaten eggs, and seasoned dried breadcrumbs.

TURN A SIMPLE GREEN SALAD into something special by topping it with a few fried oysters.

MUSTARD TARTAR SAUCE
MAKES ABOUT 1½ CUPS

This would also be a fine dipping sauce or topping for poached shellfish and fried seafood.

3 tablespoons minced dill pickles

1 tablespoon chopped capers

1 tablespoon chopped tarragon

1 tablespoon chopped flat-leaf parsley

1 cup mayonnaise

2 tablespoons freshly squeezed lime juice

1 tablespoon Dijon mustard

Fine sea salt and freshly ground black pepper

½ teaspoon mustard seeds

1. Put the pickles, capers, tarragon, and parsley in a food processor and pulse to chop them together. Add the mayonnaise, lime juice, and mustard and pulse just to combine. Season with salt and pepper.

2. To serve, spoon the sauce into a small bowl and scatter the mustard seeds over the top.

HACKED CHILE LOBSTER

THIS CASUAL, rustic dish takes lobster to a new height of flavor, lifting it from a dainty dinner to an almost primal, hands-on experience. Cooking and serving lobster in its shell retains and adds flavor by drawing intense lobster essence from the shell itself, especially when the lobster is cooked over high heat in a sauté pan as it is here. Since lobster is often an indulgence, this recipe is scaled to serve two. To prepare this dish for more, simply multiply the quantities accordingly.

1 cup loosely packed basil

4 garlic cloves

¼ cup white wine vinegar

⅓ cup plus 3 tablespoons extra virgin olive oil

Fine sea salt and freshly ground black pepper

Two 1½-pound live lobsters, rinsed with cold water

2 to 3 hot red chiles or jalapeño peppers, seeded and minced, or ½ teaspoon crushed red pepper flakes

½ cup dry white wine

3 tablespoons unsalted butter, softened at room temperature

½ cup coarsely chopped unsalted peanuts

One 8-ounce package Asian thin rice stick noodles or cellophane (bean thread) noodles, fried in 3 tablespoons hot oil until puffed

1. Put the basil in a food processor fitted with the metal blade. Pulse to begin chopping, then add the garlic and vinegar and pulse to puree. With the motor running, drizzle in ⅓ cup of the oil, season with 1 teaspoon salt and 1 teaspoon pepper, and pour into a container. Set aside.

2. Put the lobsters in a plastic bag and put them in the freezer for 20 minutes to numb them. Remove them from the freezer and use a sharp, heavy chef's knife to split the lobster in half lengthwise through the body, which will kill them instantly. Remove the claws and crack them with the blunt side of the knife. Remove the tail shell, cut it in half, and cut each half into 2 or 3 pieces. Alternatively, you can par-cook the lobster by steaming it for 6 minutes, then hacking it up. Marinate the lobster in half of the basil-garlic-vinegar puree.

REPLACE THE LOBSTER with fresh jumbo shrimp, Louisiana crawfish, or mussels, cooking all of them in their shells.

SERVE THE LOBSTER and sauce over linguine or basmati rice.

ADD SLICED CHICKEN BREAST, sautéed until brown, along with the lobster. Or add halved, blanched, shocked, and drained broccoli raab stems along with the lobster.

3. Pour the remaining 3 tablespoons oil into a large wok or heavy-bottomed sauté pan and heat it over high heat. Add the chiles, stir-fry for 30 seconds, then add the hacked lobster, in batches if necessary. Quickly stir-fry the lobster in the oil for 1 to 2 minutes, periodically splashing it with a few tablespoons of wine to help steam and flavor it. Cover the wok and let it steam for 4 to 5 minutes. The lobster is done when the shell has turned bright red and the meat is opaque.

4. Add a few tablespoons of basil puree, butter, and peanuts to the wok and stir to coat the lobster. Serve the lobster pieces with their shells on a platter or individual plates on a bed of fried noodles. Pass nutcrackers and plenty of napkins alongside.

SICILIAN SHRIMP AND COUSCOUS

SERVES 4 TO 6

WHILE COUSCOUS is often thought of as a Moroccan staple, it also has a home in Italy, especially Sicily, where the Spanish, Arab, and French influences of centuries of occupation reveal a complex blend of those cultures. Couscous, or cuscus in the Sicilian dialect, reveals the full flavor of Sicilian food in this simple dish. Couscous is traditionally steamed in a special pot over savory broth, but this recipe allows easy and successful cooking in the broth.

2 tablespoons olive oil

1 small onion, cut into small dice (about ½ cup)

Pinch of saffron threads

2 tablespoons tomato paste

Fine sea salt and freshly ground black pepper

¼ teaspoon crushed red pepper flakes, plus more to taste

2 cups bottled clam juice, enriched with shrimp shells to make a broth (see opposite page)

2 cups packaged, quick-cooking couscous, rinsed under cold

running water and drained

1 pound fresh small shrimp (about 26 shrimp), peeled and deveined, shells reserved for enriching clam juice

¼ cup shelled almonds, coarsely ground

1. Heat the oil in a large, heavy-bottomed pot over low heat. Add the onion and sauté until softened but not browned, about 4 minutes. After 1 to 2 minutes, stir in the saffron, tomato paste, ½ teaspoon salt, ½ teaspoon pepper, and pepper flakes with the onion, working quickly to avoid scorching the paste.

2. Add the clam juice to the pot, stirring it into the seasonings with a wooden spoon. Raise the heat to high and bring the liquid to a boil, then lower the heat so the liquid is simmering strongly. Pour the couscous into the simmering broth and cook until some of the liquid has been absorbed, about 2 minutes.

3. Season the shrimp with salt and pepper and stir them into the couscous and broth. Cover the pot and let the shrimp steam until firm and pink, about 4 more minutes.

4. Spoon some shrimp and couscous into individual bowls, scatter some almond over each serving, and serve at once.

Enriching shellfish broth

After peeling and deveining the shrimp, reserve the shells. Bring the clam juice to a gentle boil in a pot over medium heat, then lower the heat so the liquid is simmering. Add the reserved shrimp shells and cook together for 20 minutes before straining out the shells and any other solids. Set the stock aside and discard the shells. Keep warm, or cool, cover, and refrigerate promptly.

ANY FIRM, WHITEFISH such as sea bass, halibut, or fillet of sole, cut into cubes and poached in the broth during the final 3 to 5 minutes of cooking, would be delicious in place of the shrimp. Sicilians would choose an oily fish like mackerel.

FOR VEGETARIAN COUSCOUS, use vegetable broth instead of the clam juice and shellfish broth, and replace the shrimp with 1 cup diced zucchini and 1 cup sliced mushrooms, adding both along with the onion in step 1.

SPANISH-STYLE SQUID AND OLIVE CASSEROLE

SERVES 4 AS A MAIN COURSE

THE SPANISH *CAZUELA,* a ceramic vessel used to cook many dishes both on the stove and in the oven, was the inspiration for this dish, which proves that your muse can be anything, from an ingredient to a piece of cooking equipment. While not an authentic dish of Spain, this casserole is a great example of how freewheeling a special can be: take an influence (Spanish), a plentiful ingredient (squid), and make up something fun and fast. Serve this with Coconut-Scented Basmati Rice (page 97), Braised Kale with Red Wine (page 256), and/or Garlic-Roasted Yuca (page 242).

¼ cup olive oil

1 small onion, finely chopped (about ½ cup)

1 tablespoon chopped garlic

½ cup green Spanish olives, pitted and chopped

Pinch of saffron threads

1 tablespoon tomato paste

2 plum tomatoes, coarsely chopped

½ cup dry white wine

½ cup bottled clam juice

1 pound cleaned squid, body cut into ¼-inch-thick rings, tentacles halved crosswise

Fine sea salt and freshly ground black pepper

1. Preheat the oven to 425°F.

2. Heat the olive oil in a small, heavy-bottomed, overproof pot over medium-high heat. Add the onion and sauté until softened but not browned, about 4 minutes. Add the garlic, stir, then add the olives and cook for 2 minutes. Stir in the saffron, tomato paste, tomatoes, wine, and clam juice. Cook, stirring, for 5 minutes to bring the flavors together. Season the squid with salt and pepper before adding it to the pot and stir.

3. Put the pot in the oven and bake until the top is bubbly, 35 to 40 minutes.

4. Remove the pot from the oven, taste and adjust the seasoning with salt and pepper, transfer to a large serving bowl, and serve family style from the center of the table.

YOUR **NIGHTLY SPECIALS**

MAKE THIS WITH PEELED, DEVEINED SMALL OR MEDIUM shrimp, or assorted shellfish such as shrimp, clams, and/or mussels, leaving the clams and mussels in their shells. Or use fresh codfish, cut into large cubes.

ADD A TOTAL OF 1 CUP DICED, COOKED IDAHO OR RUSSET POTATOES, sliced roasted bell peppers, and/or sliced cured chorizo, along with the onion in step 2.

CEVICHE OF BAY SCALLOPS AND BLOOD ORANGES

SERVES 4 TO 6 AS AN APPETIZER

A CEVICHE IS A DISH in which raw fish and/or shellfish are "cooked" by the acid of citrus fruit. It's one of those great, easy ideas that lends itself to any number of interpretations. All ceviches are based on fresh fish or shellfish, an acidic marinade, and potent seasoning. They are especially successful when they feature contrasting tastes and textures such as sweet and sour, spicy and sweet, or tender and crunchy. If you're a fan of cocktails, serve this with a margarita or mojito.

Juice of 2 limes

2 blood oranges (if unavailable, substitute navel oranges or ½ cup blood orange juice, sometimes available frozen in supermarkets)

1 pound small bay scallops

1 small red onion, cut into small dice

¼ cup chopped flat-leaf parsley

2 tablespoons chopped cilantro, plus more for garnish

½ jalapeño pepper, seeded and cut into small dice

½ small red bell pepper, stemmed and seeded, cut into small dice

Fine sea salt and freshly ground black pepper

Fresh shaved coconut, for garnish

YOUR NIGHTLY SPECIALS

IF YOU CANNOT FIND BLOOD ORANGES, any orange will be fine. Consider ruby red grapefruit from Texas; its fruity sweetness approximates the flavor of a blood orange.

USE SMALL SHRIMP, lightly poached in simmering vegetable broth, instead of scallops.

1. Pour the lime juice into a bowl.

2. Peel and segment the blood oranges. Set the segments aside. Squeeze the juice out of the pulpy center into the bowl with the lime juice. Put the scallops in the bowl with the juices and let marinate for 20 to 30 minutes.

3. Drain the juice from the scallops. Add the orange segments to the bowl, along with the onion, parsley, cilantro, jalapeño, and bell pepper. Season with salt and pepper and toss gently.

4. Divide the scallops among 4 to 6 chilled glasses (martini glasses are especially festive) and pour any juice in the bowl over them. Garnish each serving with a few cilantro leaves and coconut and serve with a small spoon.

BACON-WRAPPED SEA SCALLOPS WITH WILTED LEMON SPINACH

SERVES 4 TO 6 AS AN APPETIZER

IN THE MARTINI-GLASS and lounge-music world of 1950s and 1960s cocktail parties, "angels on horseback" was one of the top ten hors d'oeuvres. It featured bacon-wrapped oysters, a perfect combination in which the salty, smoky slices add flavor and crunch to the voluptuous shellfish. I've often wondered why this recipe was never made into a real special, appropriate for the dinner table. Here it is, using scallops. You will need 8- to 10-inch wooden skewers for the scallops.

½ pound thinly sliced, fruitwood-smoked bacon, halved crosswise (1 half slice per scallop)

1 pound large sea scallops (about 10 scallops)

All-purpose flour, for dusting

Fine sea salt and freshly ground black pepper

2 tablespoons unsalted butter

2 tablespoons minced shallots

2 tablespoons small capers

¼ cup olive oil

1 pound spinach leaves, well washed in several changes of cold water, drained of excess liquid

2 tablespoons freshly squeezed lemon juice

1. Preheat the oven to 375°F.

2. Wrap a half slice of bacon around the circumference of each scallop, like a belt. Pierce the scallop through the side with a skewer to keep the bacon in place.

3. Dust each bacon-wrapped scallop with flour and season with salt and pepper.

4. Melt the butter in a 10- or 12-inch ovenproof sauté pan over medium-high heat. When the butter begins to foam, add the scallops to the pan and brown them, about 2 minutes. Turn the scallops over and add the shallots and capers to the pan. Transfer the pan to the oven and bake for 10 minutes.

NIGHTLY SPECIALS

FOR AN ALL-SEAFOOD DISH, wrap the scallops with smoked salmon.

REPLACE THE SCALLOPS with 1-inch slices of monkfish tail.

SKEWER 3 SCALLOPS on each skewer for a main course portion.

USE THIS RECIPE as a guide for making jumbo shrimp or scallops wrapped with prosciutto or pancetta, then cook and serve on skewers.

5.   Meanwhile, heat the oil in a sauté pan over medium-high heat. Add the spinach and lemon juice and sauté until the spinach is just wilted, about 2 minutes. Season the spinach with salt and pepper. Transfer the spinach to a platter and cover loosely with foil to keep it warm.

6.   Remove the pan from the oven and arrange the scallops over the spinach. Spoon the shallots and capers over the scallops and serve.

GRILLED SHRIMP KABOBS WITH CORN SALSA

SERVES 4 TO 6 AS AN APPETIZER

EVERYONE SEEMS TO ENJOY KABOBS. They're a convenience that makes it possible to grill small ingredients by skewering them to keep them from falling through the grate. The festive mood that overtakes people when kabobs are on the table is infectious. My favorite way to enjoy kabobs is at a summertime kabob party: set out the ingredients on ice, with skewers, let everyone make and grill their own, and just sit back and enjoy the show. You will need twelve to fifteen 10-inch wooden skewers, soaked in hot water for 30 minutes.

1 pound large shrimp (about 20 shrimp), peeled and deveined

1 pint cherry tomatoes

24 button mushrooms (about 10 ounces), stems trimmed

1 red bell pepper, stemmed and seeded and cut into 1-inch squares

1 yellow bell pepper, stemmed and seeded and cut into 1-inch squares

1 red onion, cut into 1-inch squares

⅓ cup olive oil

½ cup freshly squeezed lime juice

3 tablespoons soy sauce

2 tablespoons Thai chili sauce, or other hot sauce

2 teaspoons Thai fish sauce (nam pla; see page 27)

2 tablespoons finely chopped unsalted peanuts

Corn Salsa (recipe follows)

1. Assemble the skewers by skewering a shrimp, followed by a tomato, mushroom, red pepper square, yellow pepper square, and onion square. Repeat the sequence, then repeat with the remaining skewers. Set the skewers aside.

2. Stir the oil, lime juice, soy sauce, chili sauce, fish sauce, and peanuts together in a bowl.

3. Put the skewers in a flat baking dish and pour the marinade over the top. Cover with plastic wrap and refrigerate for 2 hours, or overnight. If you like, make and refrigerate the salsa overnight as well.

REPLACE THE SHRIMP with cubed chicken, pork, or lamb. Or use shrimp, chicken, and lamb together. You can also make this with cubes of steak-cut fish like tuna, swordfish, or mahi mahi.

MAKE THE KABOBS A MEAL in themselves by adding more vegetables and chunks of chicken. Serve each person two kabobs.

ADD CILANTRO and/or seeded, chopped jalapeño pepper to taste.

SERVE THE SALSA in a fresh avocado half as an appetizer.

ADD ONE OR TWO seeded, diced plum or beefsteak tomatoes.

4.   Prepare an outdoor grill for grilling, banking the coals to one side. Place the skewers over indirect heat and grill, turning, until the vegetables are nicely charred and the shrimp are firm and pink, 3 to 5 minutes per side. (To cook the shrimp indoors, preheat a grill pan over medium heat and cook, turning, as described.)

5.   To serve, put the corn salsa in a bowl and serve the skewers alongside on a platter.

CORN SALSA
MAKES 1½ CUPS SALSA

4 ears corn

1 large sweet red bell pepper, stemmed and seeded and quartered

1 garlic clove, minced

½ cup chopped flat-leaf parsley

⅓ cup olive oil

3 tablespoons white wine vinegar

Fine sea salt and freshly ground black pepper

1.   Peel back the cornhusks, remove the silk, enclose the corn once again, and grill over a hot flame until the corn begins to char at the edges, 4 to 6 minutes.

2.   Meanwhile, put the bell pepper on the grill and quickly grill and slightly char the exterior, turning to cook on all sides. Remove the bell peppers and corn from the grill and let cool. When cool, peel back the cornhusks and, using a sharp knife, remove the kernels from the cob. Discard the cob. Cut the bell pepper into julienne.

3.   Stir the corn, bell pepper, garlic, and parsley together in a bowl. Add the oil, vinegar, ½ teaspoon salt, and ½ teaspoon pepper and let marinate for 2 hours, or overnight, before serving.

PAN-ROASTED CLAMS AND MUSSELS WITH SMOKED CHILES

SERVES 4 AS A MAIN COURSE

O KAY, IT'S SUMMER. You have a craving for shellfish. You want to spend a minimum of time in the kitchen. This is the ticket: clams and mussels in a fragrant, slightly spicy sauce that can be soaked up with loaves of bread or eaten with a soup spoon. Serve this with ice-cold beer.

2 dozen fresh, live littleneck clams in their shells, scrubbed and carefully washed, clams with broken shells discarded

3 pounds fresh, live cultivated mussels in the shell, or 2 pounds New Zealand cockles in the shell,

washed in several changes of cold water, mussels with broken shells discarded

¼ cup olive oil

3 shallots, minced

2 garlic cloves, minced

1 cup dry white wine

1 cup coarsely chopped flat-leaf parsley

2 chipotle chiles in adobo, drained and chopped

Freshly ground black pepper

1. Drain the clams and mussels of any excess water.

2. Pour the oil into a large, deep, heavy-bottomed sauté pan and warm it over medium heat. When the oil is hot but not smoking, add the clams and mussels to the pan and lower the heat. Add the shallots, garlic, wine, parsley, and chiles. Cover the pan and simmer until the shells open, 5 to 6 minutes. Discard any clams and mussels that have not opened.

3. Season the contents of the pan with pepper and serve in bowls, topping each serving with the pan broth.

SERVE THIS OVER LINGUINE or fettuccine as a first course, or over plain white rice for a main course.

ADD ½ CUP CLAM JUICE and 1 cup canned, crushed plum tomatoes to make this more of a soup. Put a slice of toasted country bread in the bottom of each bowl and spoon some of the soup over it for a variation on a Tuscan bread soup.

LEAVE OUT THE OIL and start the dish by sautéing diced, smoked pork or spicy Spanish or Italian sausage until they render enough fat to coat the pan, then proceed with the recipe.

ON THE

Finfish from Sea to Stream

LINE

Here in New York City, I find inspiration in places like the Fulton Fish Market, one of the greatest markets in the world and a sort of culinary Brigadoon: it materializes every night and disappears every dawn. The market is a metaphor for the melting pot that is New York, as there are fish for every ethnic group and every budget.

Because of markets like this, coast-dwellers like myself tend to take fresh fish for granted. We write recipes and talk about fish and shellfish as though everyone in the country can just stroll down the street and into a corner fish store. But what once might have seemed an unrealistic view of the world today is pretty realistic: in this age of supersonic flights and sophisticated technology, it is possible to get fresh fish just about anywhere. If you are a home cook for whom fresh fish is less readily available, remember that the more you ask for it in your local market, the more likely it is that the retailer will respond by stocking more and better varieties of fresh seafood.

Cooking fish shouldn't pose any mystery to cooks. We should be as unafraid to cook fish as we are a cut of meat. But, as with shellfish, there's an innate fear built into the special nature of fish. The same fragility that makes them alluring to eat also makes them intimidating to cook. We fear we'll overcook it, undercook it, or just plain make it badly.

As with shellfish, you should seek out the freshest fish possible, and that may not be the one you originally set out to buy. Be flexible at the market, and ask your reputable fish butcher, looking her straight in the eye, not wavering in your stare: ". . . in all honesty, what is the freshest fish you have today? Tell me, what was its place of origin? Was it ever frozen? Would you serve it to your own mother?" Most of those who deal in fresh fish and seafood take their noble and ancient profession quite seriously; they will respect your earnest questions and try to be helpful.

Store all fish refrigerated and well chilled and do not allow it to come into contact with other foods. Use or freeze all fish and seafood as soon as possible after purchasing. All fish should be wrapped in clean plastic wrap or food wrapping paper and kept in the coldest part of your refrigerator. In hot weather, store wrapped fish on ice in one of the vegetable compartments in the bottom of the fridge. When preparing recipes that require fish to sit out at room temperature for extended periods during preparation, keep it in its wrapping or container on ice while handling and preparing other ingredients.

Avoid already cut fillets sold and wrapped in the refrigerated section of many markets, depriving you of the chance to observe some of the key freshness indicators of whole fish: clear rather than milky or clouded eyes, red or pinkish colored gills, and a spongy feel to the flesh.

PAN-ROASTED HALIBUT WITH ASPARAGUS, FAVA BEANS, AND THYME BROTH

SERVES 4 AS A MAIN COURSE

Halibut is only fished on the Atlantic and Pacific coasts, but it's become a real star on restaurant menus just about everywhere in between. Its combination of firm, white flesh and mild flavor makes it rewarding even when simply prepared. This dish celebrates the spring, using the sweet halibut as a backdrop to the grassiness of asparagus and the earthy favas. If you like, serve the halibut on top of Mashed Potatoes (page 236) and spoon the vegetables and broth over and around it.

Fine sea salt and freshly ground black pepper

½ cup shelled fava beans (see page 148), from 1 pound beans in the pod

¾ pound pencil asparagus, tips cut into 1-inch pieces, stems cut into bite-size pieces

3 tablespoons olive oil

1½ pounds skinless, boneless, ¾-inch-thick halibut fillet, cut into 4 pieces

3 tablespoons thinly sliced shallots

¼ cup dry white wine (preferably Chardonnay)

½ cup homemade vegetable stock (page 65) or low-sodium, store-bought vegetable broth

3 tablespoons unsalted butter

3 tablespoons chopped thyme or flat-leaf parsley, plus a few sprigs for garnish

1. Preheat the oven to 450°F.

2. Bring a large pot of salted water to a boil over high heat. Fill a large bowl halfway with ice water.

3. Remove the beans from the pod. Add the fava beans to the boiling water and cook for 1 minute. Use a slotted spoon to transfer the beans to the ice water. As soon as they are cool enough to handle, remove from the water, then peel off and discard the coating. Set the favas aside.

NIGHTLY SPECIALS

THE VEGETABLE MIXTURE can be augmented or totally changed. Add sliced cremini mushrooms to the pan with the minced shallots in step 6 and cook them until they begin to give off their liquid. Use French green beans in place of or in addition to the fava beans and/or asparagus.

FOR A RICHER DISH, drizzle some extra virgin olive oil over each serving.

4. Add the asparagus stems and tips to the boiling water and cook for 3 minutes. Drain and transfer to the ice water to shock them and set their color. Drain and set aside.

5. Pour the oil into a wide, heavy-bottomed, ovenproof sauté pan and heat it over medium-high heat. Season the halibut with salt and pepper. Add the fish to the pan, flesh side down, and sauté until golden brown, about 4 minutes. Turn the fillets over and put the pan in the oven for 6 minutes.

6. Remove the pan from the oven, use a spatula to set the fish aside on a plate, and return the pan to the stovetop over medium-high heat. Add the shallots to the pan, then pour in the wine and broth, raise the heat to high, bring to a boil, and let boil until slightly reduced, about 3 minutes. Add the fava beans, asparagus, and butter and cook until the butter melts and thickens the broth and the vegetables are warmed through, about 1 minute. Season with salt and pepper and stir in the thyme.

7. Put 1 fillet in the center of each of 4 wide, shallow bowls and spoon some thyme broth, asparagus, and fava beans over the top. Garnish with a few thyme sprigs and serve.

Fava beans

Fresh fava beans are a thumbnail-size pulse that needs to be removed from its heavy outer shell-pod casing before cooking. Generally speaking, each 4- to 6-inch shell holds 6 to 8 beans. Each bean is encased in a thin outer coating that also must be removed. Dried fava beans are also available, ready to be cooked like dried beans.

PAN-FRIED GROUPER WITH PAPAYA RELISH AND CHILI OIL

SERVES 4 TO 6

Bᴀᴛᴛᴇʀɪɴɢ ᴀɴᴅ ꜰʀʏɪɴɢ is often leaned on as a way to use unspecified white fish in sea shack–type settings, or in regional specialties like fish and chips in England or fish tacos in Mexico. This dish takes fried fish to another level by using a quality catch and pairing it with something less predictable than tartar sauce or malt vinegar. A combination of breadcrumbs and cornmeal creates a crispy coating that lets you really appreciate the grouper's texture. Serve this with Mango and Red Onion Salad with Basil Vinaigrette (page 13).

1 small papaya (about ½ pound), peeled, halved, seeded (see opposite page), and sliced crosswise into ¼-inch slices

¼ cup light brown sugar

Juice of 2 limes

1 small red onion, cut into small dice (about ½ cup)

1 small red bell pepper, stemmed and seeded, cut into small dice (about ½ cup)

1 small hot chile, such as jalapeño, seeded and minced, optional

1 cup all-purpose flour

2 eggs

½ cup milk

2 tablespoons plus ¼ cup vegetable oil

1 cup dried breadcrumbs

1½ cups cornmeal

2 teaspoons Spanish smoked paprika or regular paprika

Fine sea salt and freshly ground black pepper

1½ pounds skinless, boneless grouper fillet

2 tablespoons chili oil (available in supermarket Asian food sections), optional

1. Stir the papaya, brown sugar, lime juice, onion, bell pepper, and chile, if using, together in a small bowl. Let marinate while you prepare the grouper or, if preparing in advance, overnight. Let come to room temperature before serving.

2. Use the classic three-dish arrangement for the breading process: a separate dish for each of the three elements of breading, preferably flat and

INSTEAD OF GROUPER, use red snapper, sea bass, flounder, or codfish.

INSTEAD OF THE PAPAYA RELISH, use diced mango, chopped orange segments, diced avocado, Mustard Tartar Sauce (page 126), or Corn Salsa (page 141) to complement the fish and coating.

MAKE A PAPAYA-STRAWBERRY SMOOTHIE with 1 cup peeled, diced papaya; ½ cup strawberries; ½ cup milk; and ½ cup plain yogurt. Blend all the ingredients with 2 cups ice until smooth for 2 to 4 smoothies. Serve the smoothie with this dish.

with 1- to 2-inch sides to hold the ingredients and make it easy to dip the fish in them. Put the flour in one dish, beat the eggs and milk with the 2 tablespoons vegetable oil in another dish, and mix the breadcrumbs, cornmeal, and paprika with 1 teaspoon salt and 1 teaspoon pepper in the third.

3. Cut the grouper into 4 equal portions and season with salt and pepper. Dip and dredge the grouper pieces one at a time through the flour, then dip into the egg mix, and finally dredge in the breading. Set the fish on a plate, cover with plastic wrap, and refrigerate until ready to proceed. This may be done up to 4 hours ahead of time; let come to room temperature before proceeding.

4. Pour the ¼ cup vegetable oil into a large, heavy-bottomed sauté pan and heat it over medium heat. Add the breaded fish and cook, turning once, until the fish is golden brown all over but still moist inside, 4 to 5 minutes per side, depending on the thickness.

5. Put a heaping spoonful of the papaya relish in the center of each of 4 to 6 plates. Set a fried grouper fillet on top of the relish, drizzle the chili oil, if using, around the plate, and serve.

Papaya

Use a sharp paring knife to peel papaya. Discard the skin, cut the fruit in half lengthwise, and use a teaspoon to scoop out the small black seeds. Papayas are often very large; store fully ripened, softened papaya in the refrigerator.

FLORIBBEAN-STYLE TILEFISH PAN-FRIED WITH LIMES, CHILES, TOMATOES, AND AVOCADO

SERVES 4 AS A MAIN COURSE

No, THAT ISN'T A TYPO: Floribbean is a way of referring to the combination Floridian-Caribbean cooking style of this recipe where tilefish, limes, and tomato meet with fiery spices and cream. It was actually inspired as a nightly special by another chef, Norman Van Aken, the renowned South Florida talent whose New World cooking unites contemporary techniques with traditional, regional flavors. I was so impressed by his inventive use of the ingredients available to him in his tropical home that I devised this recipe in the spirit of the menu he served on the night I dined in his restaurant.

Tilefish, once a relatively unpopular Atlantic species, has become so popular in recent years that it is in high demand, especially in relation to its limited supply. So it can be hard to find but is well worth the effort. Note the very useful technique for making the sauce, which is sort of a foolproof beurre blanc (butter and white wine sauce) emulsified with cream to keep it from separating. Serve this with Coconut-Scented Basmati Rice (page 97).

3 tablespoons olive oil

2 shallots, thinly sliced

3 garlic cloves, crushed, plus 1 clove, minced

½ jalapeño pepper, seeded and finely diced

2 tablespoons coriander seeds

1 tablespoon ground cumin

1 teaspoon crushed red pepper flakes

2 cups dry white wine

3 tablespoons freshly squeezed lime juice

Four 8-ounce tilefish fillets (¾ inch thick)

Fine sea salt and freshly ground black pepper

¼ cup heavy cream

4 tablespoons (½ stick) very cold unsalted butter, cut in pieces

2 large fresh beefsteak tomatoes, peeled, seeded, and diced (see page 123)

2 tablespoons chopped cilantro

1 firm, ripe avocado, diced (see page 24)

IF YOU CAN'T FIND TILEFISH make this with grouper, mahi mahi, mackerel, or swordfish.

TAKE THIS RECIPE IN A MEDITERRANEAN DIRECTION by leaving out the cumin and coriander and adding several sprigs of thyme, oregano, and rosemary to the wine before reducing. Finish the butter sauce with additional fresh herbs.

1.   Put 1 tablespoon of the oil, the shallots, crushed garlic, jalapeño, coriander, cumin, pepper flakes, 1¾ cups of the wine, and the lime juice in a saucepan and bring to a simmer over medium heat. Continue to simmer until reduced to ⅓ cup, about 10 minutes.

2.   Meanwhile, pour the remaining 2 tablespoons olive oil into a large, heavy-bottomed sauté pan and set it over medium-high heat. Season the fish with salt and pepper. Add the fish to the hot oil and cook until golden, 3 to 4 minutes, then turn and cook the other side until golden, about 3 more minutes. Transfer the fish to a plate. (Don't put the pan in the sink; you'll need it again in a minute.)

3.   Pour the cream into the simmering mixture, return to a simmer over low heat, and continue to simmer until reduced slightly, about 2 minutes. Remove the pan from the heat and whisk in the cold butter. Strain through a fine-mesh strainer into a bowl, discard the solids, and cover the butter sauce to keep warm.

4.   To the still-hot fish pan, add the tomatoes and sauté for 2 minutes, then add the minced garlic, cilantro, and remaining ¼ cup wine. Cook for 1 minute. Add the avocado and remove the pan from the heat immediately.

5.   Mound some of the tomato-avocado mixture in the center of each of 4 dinner plates or wide, shallow bowls. Set a fish steak atop each mound and drizzle the butter sauce over and around the fish.

STEAMED BASS WITH LEMONGRASS AND CHILE-COCONUT BROTH

SERVES 4 AS A MAIN COURSE

For DECADES NOW, *steaming has been one of the preferred cooking techniques of the health- and weight-conscious, which might explain why even accomplished home cooks overlook it as an effective way to transmit flavor to vegetables, fish, and poultry. Steaming cooks fish so cleanly, without the use of butter or oil, that even captured in vapor, the flavor of the aromatic ingredients take to the fish here. And steaming is less aggressive than even poaching would be, though this aromatic broth could be used as a poaching liquid. Serve Gingered Green Beans (page 260) alongside this dish. You will need a bamboo basket steamer.*

½ cup bottled clam juice

½ cup dry sherry

2 tablespoons plus 2 teaspoons soy sauce

½ cup unsweetened coconut milk

2 or 3 lemongrass stalks, crushed (see page 156)

2 tablespoons peeled, minced ginger

1 dried chile or ¼ teaspoon crushed red pepper flakes

¼ cup chopped scallions, plus more for serving

12 large shiitake mushrooms, stems removed and discarded

1 small bok choy, halved and sliced lengthwise into wedges

1 tablespoon Thai red curry paste, or to taste (many supermarket brands are available)

Lettuce leaves, for lining the steamer basket

Four 8-ounce boneless sea bass or striped bass fillets, skin on

Fine sea salt and freshly ground black pepper

Coconut-Scented Basmati Rice (page 97)

1. Pour the clam juice, sherry, soy sauce, and coconut milk into a heavy-bottomed sauté pan or pot the same diameter as your bamboo steaming basket and bring the mixture to a boil over high heat. Reduce the heat so the liquid is simmering and add the lemongrass, ginger, chile, scallions, mushrooms, bok choy, and curry paste. Continue to simmer gently for 15 minutes to let the flavors mingle.

PERCH, TILAPIA, AND FLOUN-
DER all steam very well and can
be used instead of sea bass. You
can also make this with shrimp
and/or scallops. Cooking times
vary, based on the size of the
shellfish.

THE STEAMING TECHNIQUE
has almost endless applications.
For example, you can take this
dish in a Southwestern direction
by omitting the coconut milk,
lemongrass, and ginger, adding
some cider vinegar, crumbling a
dried chipotle pepper into the
broth, and adding 1 teaspoon
ground cumin. Serve the fish as it
is here, passing flour tortillas
alongside. Pair this version with
Corn Salsa (page 141).

2. Arrange a layer of lettuce leaves in the steamer basket to keep the fish from touching the raw bamboo. Season the fillets with salt and pepper and arrange them on the lettuce in the steamer. Set the steamer over the simmering liquid, cover with the bamboo cover, lower the heat, and steam gently until the fish is cooked through, 8 to 9 minutes.

3. Remove the steamer from the pot. Use tongs to remove the bok choy and mushrooms from the liquid and divide them decoratively among 4 dinner plates or wide, shallow bowls. Arrange the fish fillets on top of the vegetables on each plate. Pass the rice family style from the bowl.

4. Use tongs to fish out and discard the lemongrass and ladle a little of the broth over the fish on each plate. Scatter some scallions over each serving and serve.

Lemongrass

The bulb end is where most of the flavorful and aromatic volatile oils are to be found. Just give a sharp, crushing rap with the flat of a knife to release them.

RED SNAPPER WITH LITTLENECK CLAMS AND TOMATOES

SERVES 4

RED SNAPPER IS *one of the finest eating fish that's commonly available. If it's not available, make this with farm-raised striped bass, which bears little resemblance, in both size (much smaller) and flavor (more subtle), to wild striped bass. But it does have the charm of being regularly available, clean tasting, and versatile.*

2 tablespoons olive oil

1 tablespoon unsalted butter

1½ pounds red snapper fillet, cut into 4 pieces

Fine sea salt and freshly ground black pepper

2 garlic cloves, minced

½ pound ripe plum tomatoes, peeled (page 123), seeded, and chopped (about 1½ cups)

20 basil leaves, cut into julienne

1 cup dry white wine

12 littleneck clams in their shells, scrubbed under cold running water

1. Heat the olive oil and butter in a heavy-bottomed sauté pan with a lid over medium heat. Season the fish with salt and pepper. Add the fish, skin side down, to the pan and cook over medium heat until browned on both sides, about 3 minutes per side. Transfer the fish to a plate and cover with foil to keep warm.

2. Add the garlic to the pan and sauté for 1 minute. Add the tomatoes and cook for 2 minutes. Add the basil and wine and bring to a boil over high heat, then lower the heat so the liquid is simmering.

3. Return the fish to the pan, resting it on top of the tomatoes. Scatter the clams around the fish, cover the pan with a lid, and steam until the clams open, about 3 minutes. Discard any clams that have not opened.

4. Divide the fish, clams, and broth among 4 rimmed plates or bowls and serve.

YOUR NIGHTLY SPECIALS

INSTEAD OF SNAPPER, use sea trout or orange roughy.

USE MUSSELS instead of clams; cook them for 1 or 2 minutes longer.

SCATTER A TEASPOON OF CHOPPED FRESH HERBS like oregano and/or parsley over each portion just before serving.

FINISH EACH SERVING with a drizzle of extra virgin olive oil and/or lemon juice.

ADD CHILES to the broth.

ADD A TABLESPOON OF PEELED, MINCED GINGER and a dash of soy sauce to the broth.

GRILLED MARINATED SWORDFISH WITH FIRE-ROASTED PEPPERS AND FRESH HERB VINAIGRETTE

SERVES 4

THIS DISH IS DOMINATED by the flavors of capers, pureed here with parsley, lemon juice, and garlic into a pesto-like fish marinade. I tasted a similar dish in a local home during a visit to a Mediterranean caper farm. It gave me a new appreciation for this salty staple, and I promise it will do the same for you. Once marinated, the fish is grilled and paired with charred onions and peppers, then topped with a light, herbaceous vinaigrette.

⅓ cup plus 3 tablespoons olive oil

Juice of 3 lemons (about ¼ cup)

2 garlic cloves

¼ cup lightly packed flat-leaf parsley

1 tablespoon capers (preferably salt-packed), rinsed and drained

Four 6- to 8-ounce swordfish steaks (at least ¾ inch thick)

2 large Vidalia onions, halved and sliced into ¼-inch-thick slices

2 red bell peppers, stemmed and seeded and thinly sliced into rings

2 yellow bell peppers, stemmed and seeded and thinly sliced into rings

Fine sea salt and freshly ground black pepper

Fresh Herb Vinaigrette (recipe follows)

1. Make the marinade: put ⅓ cup of the oil, the lemon juice, garlic, parsley, and capers in a food processor fitted with the steel blade. Pulse until coarsely chopped, then transfer to a bowl.

2. Rub the swordfish steaks with the marinade. Set them in a baking dish or other vessel capable of holding them in a single layer, cover with plastic wrap, and refrigerate for 1 to 2 hours.

3. Prepare an outdoor grill for cooking or preheat a grill pan over high heat.

USE TUNA OR MAHI MAHI instead of swordfish; both stand up well to grilling and to the potent marinade.

MAKE THIS AN APPETIZER by using smaller steaks, omitting the vegetables, and setting each steak on a bed of greens after grilling.

ADD AS MANY TYPES OF VEGETABLES as you like, the more variety the better. Some recommendations: portobello mushroom caps, sliced zucchini, sliced yellow squash, and sliced eggplant.

4.   Just before grilling, put the onions and peppers in a bowl. Drizzle with the remaining 3 tablespoons oil and season with salt and pepper. Toss well.

5.   When the grill is hot, put the swordfish steaks in the center of the grill without crowding and use tongs to spread the vegetables out around the edge, taking care to lay each one down horizontally so it doesn't fall through the grate. Cook the swordfish until it is well marked on both sides (turn to rotate the grill marks) and the interior is medium, 3 to 4 minutes per side.

6.   Remove the vegetables and fish from the grill and arrange them on a platter, topping them with the fish. Drizzle the vinaigrette over and around the fish and vegetables and serve.

FRESH HERB VINAIGRETTE
MAKES ABOUT ¾ CUP

Use this vinaigrette to top fish, poultry, and sliced, roasted, or grilled pork.

¼ cup balsamic vinegar

1 tablespoon Dijon mustard

2 tablespoons chopped thyme

2 tablespoons chopped oregano

8 large basil leaves

¾ cup extra virgin olive oil

Fine sea salt and freshly ground black pepper

Put the vinegar and mustard in a food processor fitted with the steel blade. Pulse briefly, then add the herbs. Pulse again until coarsely chopped. With the processor running, add the olive oil very slowly so that the mixture emulsifies into a smooth blend. Season with salt and pepper. This dressing will keep for up to 3 days in the refrigerator.

PEPPER-CRUSTED TUNA WITH GREEN OLIVE SAUCE

SERVES 4

ONE OF THE FIRST SPECIALS I offered when I was a sous chef at '21' was a peppered tuna steak. Believe it or not, it was something of a novelty back then. I served it with a bracing tomato relish and buttered green beans. This recipe, based on that one, is a real pantry special, if you count your bar as part of your pantry: the key ingredients—olive, gin, and vermouth—are the essential components of a martini. The stir-fry of carrots and chayote is intended to add snap and crunch, like the peanuts or pretzels you might snack on with a cocktail.

Be careful not to overcook fresh tuna. Let it come to room temperature just before cooking so the inside can be cooked rare or medium-rare without drying out.

1 cup fresh breadcrumbs, pulsed to fine in a food processor

3 tablespoons coarsely ground black pepper

Four 6-ounce skinless tuna steaks (¾ inch thick)

¼ cup olive oil

1 whole chayote, julienned (see page 164; zucchini or yellow squash can be substituted)

1 small carrot, peeled and cut into julienne

3 tablespoons minced shallots

16 martini olives, pitted, drained, and sliced crosswise

3 thyme sprigs

¼ cup gin

¼ cup dry vermouth

½ cup homemade chicken stock (page 69) or store-bought, low-sodium chicken broth

3 tablespoons unsalted butter

Fine sea salt

1. Stir the breadcrumbs and pepper together in a bowl. Spread the mixture out on a large plate. Coat the tuna with the mixture by pressing all sides of each steak on the plate, pressing down so the coating adheres.

2. Heat the oil in a heavy-bottomed sauté pan over medium heat. Cook the tuna in the pan without crowding until golden brown, about 2 min-

INSTEAD OF GREEN OLIVES, use Kalamata olives for an intense salty flavor or blanched pearl onions for another alternative.

REPLACE THE GIN and vermouth with white wine or tequila, and finish the sauce with a teaspoon or so each of oregano and parsley.

utes. Turn the steaks over and cook on the other side for about 2 minutes for rare, 3 for medium-rare. Remove the tuna to a plate and cover loosely with foil to keep warm. Set aside.

3. Add the chayote to the pan, raise the heat to high, and wilt for 1 minute. Add the carrot and cook for 2 minutes. Add the shallots, olives, thyme, gin, and vermouth, stir to combine, and cook for 1 minute. Pour in the broth, bring to a boil, and let boil for 1 minute to reduce slightly. Stir in the butter, season with salt and pepper, and remove the pan from the heat. Use tongs or a slotted spoon to remove and discard the thyme sprigs.

4. To serve, slice each tuna steak in half. Arrange some of the sautéed vegetables in the center of each of 4 plates and stack 2 steak halves on top. Drizzle some sauce around the fish on each plate and serve.

Chayote

Chayote, or mirliton, is a crisp vegetable used extensively in New Orleans and Caribbean cooking. It looks like a pear and cooks like a zucchini, but stays firm, not mushy. It can be eaten raw or cooked and is especially good in stews.

MONKFISH "OSSO BUCO" WITH PANCETTA AND CARROTS

SERVES 4

THERE ARE FEW MORE SUREFIRE WAYS *of pleasing a crowd than with a playful variation on a classic dish. This is a seafood variation of osso buco (the name means "hole in the bone"), an Italian classic in which a veal shank is braised for hours. The orange zest–parsley mixture that tops each serving is a play on gremolata, the chopped parsley, garlic, and lemon zest that tops a traditional osso buco.*

Four 8-ounce monkfish tails (1½ inches thick), on the bone (see page 167)

½ cup all-purpose flour

Fine sea salt and freshly ground black pepper

¼ cup oil

½ pound pancetta, minced

2 medium onions, cut into small dice

1 medium carrot, cut into small dice

½ fennel bulb, cut into small dice, fronds reserved

2 garlic cloves

1 cup dry white wine

½ cup chopped plum tomatoes

1 cup flat-leaf parsley

2 tablespoons grated orange zest

1. Coat the monkfish with flour and season with salt and pepper. Set aside.

2. Heat the oil in a 2-inch-high, heavy-bottomed sauté pan with a cover over medium-high heat. Set the monkfish tails in the pan without crowding and sear on one side until golden brown, about 2 minutes. Turn them over, add the pancetta to the pan, and sear the tails on the other side for 2 minutes. Use a spatula to remove the fish and pancetta to a plate and cover with foil to keep them warm.

3. Add the onions, carrots, fennel, and garlic to the pan and sauté over high heat, stirring, to begin caramelizing the vegetables, 5 to 8 minutes.

THIS DISH IS SO SPECIAL with monkfish that I hesitate to offer any alternatives. But you can make it with mahi mahi steaks, yellowtail steaks, or salmon fillets.

IF YOU'RE NOT A MEAT-EATER, just leave out the pancetta.

SERVE THIS OVER RISOTTO (page 102).

Spread the vegetables over the surface of the pan and set the fish and pancetta over them. Pour the wine and tomatoes into the pan, raise the heat, and bring to a boil. Lower the heat so the liquid is simmering, cover the pan, and simmer for 12 minutes.

4.   Meanwhile, put the parsley and orange zest in a food processor fitted with the steel blade. Pulse until finely chopped. Transfer the mixture to a bowl and set aside.

5.   Transfer 1 monkfish tail to the center of each of 4 dinner plates. Top with some of the vegetables and sauce and finish with the orange-parsley mixture and some fennel fronds.

Monkfish

Monkfish has an unusual shape, to say the least. Its tail is enormous and seems to flow right into the head. Monkfish are always sold sans head, which are used for bait. Consequently, monkfish are sold by the "tail." For this recipe, ask your fishmonger for smaller tails with the skin removed but have the fish cut like a steak, directly through the bone, leaving a center bone with two "fillets" of fish on either side. A 3- to 4-inch piece with two fillets on each side of the bone is a good size.

GRILLED WISCONSIN WHITEFISH SALAD WITH YELLOW TOMATO AND TARRAGON VINAIGRETTE

SERVES 6

THIS WAS ANOTHER ONE of my nightly specials at '21'. Shortly after I became the chef at this great restaurant, I developed a relationship with a purveyor of whitefish freshly harvested from Lake Superior by descendents of the Ojibway tribe who exercised their federal fishing rights to earn their living. Once a week I received fish from them by overnight express that was so fresh and clean in smell and appearance that it was almost shocking how far it had traveled and yet remained just-caught fresh.

At '21', I did something different with the fish every week, but this recipe was my favorite. The key here is the freshness and quality of the ingredients: the moist, sweet flavor of perfectly cooked fish with a crispy skin and moist interior, the ripest tomatoes, in-season herbs, and the fragrance of high-quality oil and vinegar.

Four 6-ounce whitefish fillets, ideally Lake Superior whitefish, skin on, all bones removed

Canola oil, for grilling

Fine sea salt and freshly ground black pepper

2 cups mesclun salad mix

1 cup halved yellow pear tomatoes

1 cup halved red pear tomatoes

¼ cup extra virgin olive oil

1 tablespoon good-quality balsamic vinegar

2 tablespoons chopped tarragon

1 tablespoon chopped capers

Chive batons, for garnish

1. Prepare an outdoor grill for cooking, letting the coals burn until covered with white ash. Set a fish-friendly grate over the grill.

2. Brush each fish fillet with 1 teaspoon canola oil, season with salt and pepper, and lay flesh side down on the grill. Cook for 4 to 6 minutes, turn

NIGHTLY SPECIALS

YOUR

THOUGH LOW-ACID YELLOW TOMATOES are ideal here, you can substitute whatever variety of small tomatoes is readily available such as red pear, currant, or cherry.

TROUT FILLETS are a good, readily available freshwater alternative to whitefish. This recipe is also well suited to fresh salmon steaks or swordfish steaks. Arctic char, a gustatory cross between trout and salmon that tastes more like a freshwater fish would be a unique choice.

REPLACE THE BALSAMIC VINEGAR with equal parts apple cider vinegar and sharp mustard and use fresh dill in place of tarragon. Or use the Fresh Herb Vinaigrette (page 161).

over onto the skin side, and grill until crispy, another 4 to 6 minutes. (If an outdoor grill is unavailable, cook in a nonstick, stovetop grill pan, following the same directions.)

3.   As the fish is cooking, divide the greens among 6 small plates. In a small bowl, toss together the tomatoes, olive oil, vinegar, tarragon, and capers. Season with salt and pepper.

4.   As soon as the fish is done, place a fillet on top of each salad mound so that the heat of the fish warms the greens. Use a slotted spoon to divide the tomatoes among the 6 plates, then drizzle some of the vinaigrette over the top. Garnish with chive batons and serve immediately.

RAINBOW TROUT WITH SAGE-BUTTER STUFFING

SERVES 4

STUFFING DOESN'T ALWAYS MEAN TURKEY and doesn't always include bread. Here, a sage-butter stuffing is cooked in the cavity of a whole boneless trout, melting into the fish and enriching it with flavor. If you fish where keeping is permitted, using your own fresh-caught fish would make this extra special.

3 tablespoons chopped sage

4 tablespoons (½ stick) unsalted butter, softened at room temperature

Juice of 1 lemon

Fine sea salt and freshly ground black pepper

½ teaspoon paprika

3 scallions, finely chopped

½ cup dried breadcrumbs

¼ cup pine nuts, toasted in a sauté pan until fragrant

4 butterflied whole rainbow trout, skin on, bones removed (they are usually sold this way)

Olive oil

1. Preheat the oven to 375°F.

2. At least 1 hour before you plan to cook the fish, prepare the stuffing. Combine the sage, butter, lemon juice, ½ teaspoon salt, ½ teaspoon pepper, paprika, scallions, breadcrumbs, and pine nuts in a food processor fitted with the steel blade and pulse to combine well. Transfer the stuffing to a bowl, cover, and refrigerate until ready to use.

3. Season the trout with salt and pepper and rub the skin with the oil.

4. Divide the stuffing among the fish, spreading an even layer inside the cavities. Fold the fish closed to seal in the stuffing. Lay the fish in an oiled roasting pan. Roast until the fish is thoroughly cooked, 15 to 18 minutes.

USE MILD, WHITE-FLESHED FILLETS like bass, flounder, or grey sole instead of trout. In fillet form, these fish can be rolled around the stuffing, pierced with a toothpick, and roasted.

ADD MASHED ROASTED GARLIC CLOVES to the stuffing.

About halfway through the cooking time, carefully run a spatula under each trout to ensure it doesn't stick to the pan.

5. Put 1 trout on each of 4 dinner plates. Drizzle any juices and melted butter from the pan over the fish and serve.

COLD POACHED SALMON AND MARKET HERB SAUCE

SERVES 6 TO 8

THIS IS A VERY OLD-FASHIONED DISH, but it's one that a lot of people adore. When I think of it, I envision grand old hotel restaurants or posh clubs. You'll never believe this, but I was once asked to prepare a buffet dinner for The Who, a rock and roll fantasy come true. To my amazement, the band requested this dish: a classic of French and English cooking. Pair this with the Cool Roasted Beets with Mint (page 9) for a refreshing first course.

½ cup dry white wine

1 small onion, cut into small dice

3 bay leaves

1 lemon, quartered, plus 3 tablespoons freshly squeezed lemon juice

2 pounds skinless, boneless salmon, cut crosswise into 6 to 8 equal pieces (1 piece per person; cut the fish down the center line, then cut each piece into 3 or 4 pieces)

1 cup mayonnaise

½ cup watercress

½ cup flat-leaf parsley

¼ cup dill sprigs

¼ cup basil, optional

3 tablespoons tarragon, optional

Fine sea salt and freshly ground black pepper

1. Put the wine, onion, bay leaves, lemon, and 4 cups water into a heavy-bottomed pot wide enough to hold all of the fish pieces in a single layer. Bring the liquid to a boil over high heat, then lower the heat until the liquid is simmering. Add the fish to the liquid and gently poach for about 6 minutes; the first sign of white droplets issuing from the fish (the protein escaping) indicates doneness.

2. Turn off the heat and allow the fish to cool in the poaching liquid for about 30 minutes. This will ensure fully cooked but not overcooked fish.

NIGHTLY SPECIALS

FILLET OF SOLE can also be poached and served in this manner. Though unconventional choices, Arctic char or sea trout are good alternatives, as is wild striped bass if you're lucky enough to put your hands on it: now *that* would be special.

3. Meanwhile, make the sauce: Put the mayonnaise, lemon juice, watercress, parsley, dill, and basil and tarragon, if using, in a food processor fitted with the metal blade. Process until smooth. Scrape the sauce into a bowl and season with salt and pepper.

4. Using a spatula or two, transfer 1 fish piece to each of 6 to 8 cold or cool plates and top with a dollop of sauce.

SLOW-ROASTED SESAME SALMON WITH GINGER

SERVES 4

CRUSTS LIKE *herbed breadcrumbs, mustard butter, or chile and spice mixes seal in juices and keep food moist while imparting flavor and texture, as the sesame seeds do here. Serve with pickled ginger, Asian chili sauce, and additional soy sauce on the side.*

Four 6-to 7-ounce skinless salmon fillets

2 tablespoons canola oil

¼ cup white and/or black sesame seeds

2 large shallots, minced (about ¼ cup)

1 tablespoon peeled, grated ginger

1 teaspoon chili oil (available in supermarket Asian food sections)

¼ cup dry sherry wine or Spanish sherry vinegar

½ cup bottled clam juice

2 tablespoons soy sauce

Fine sea salt and freshly ground black pepper

YOUR NIGHTLY SPECIALS

USE SEA BASS, codfish, or red snapper instead of salmon.

MAKE A CRUST of ½ cup dried breadcrumbs, ½ cup crushed corn tortillas, and 2 tablespoons chili powder.

1. Preheat the oven to 350°F.

2. Brush the salmon steaks with some of the oil. Put the sesame seeds in a flat dish or pan, dredge the flesh side (not the skin side) of the steaks in the sesame seeds, and set aside.

3. Combine the shallots, ginger, chili oil, sherry, clam juice, and soy sauce in an ovenproof dish. Season the salmon steaks with salt and pepper.

4. Heat the remaining canola oil in a heavy-bottomed sauté pan over medium heat. Add the steaks to the pan and sear to a golden brown on both sides, about 2 minutes per side, taking care not to burn the sesame seeds. Put the seared fish, sesame seeds up, on the seasoned shallots in the baking dish and put the salmon in the oven. Roast for 6 minutes for medium rare or until the fish is cooked to your preference. Serve the salmon immediately.

WINGING IT

Poultry

Urban shoppers once had to flock to ethnic markets to find high-quality poultry for home cooking. But today, even if you shop in supermarkets or upscale food shops there's a wider selection of poultry from which to choose than ever before. We can all find organic, free-range, and hormone-free poultry, no matter where we live. Poultry raised in this manner tastes better, and in most cases choosing these birds over mass-produced ones is literally a choice between flavor and no flavor at all. In comparison to naturally raised birds, the big-name brands seem washed out and bland.

Whatever your source, think fresh rather than frozen when buying and cooking poultry. I always recommend buying enough to have leftovers because so many poultry dishes taste even better the next day, whether served in the same way again, or as the basis of a sandwich or salad.

Check poultry for any freshness dating on the package and select the latest date possible. Look for poultry that is kept at near freezing but not below 32°F. However it's presented at the market, it's likely that the poultry was shipped on ice by wholesalers, so make sure the cavity isn't holding any ice. Poultry skin should be free of tears, blemishes, blood, or clotting; the package should be dry, without excessive water or blood; the flesh shouldn't look old or gray, but rather should have a healthy white to pink color. In addition to your eyes, your nose is an excellent judge of freshness. Chicken should smell fresh and clean.

Even if I plan to use just one or two parts of a bird for a recipe, I often buy whole birds and cut them up myself. Knowing firsthand how fresh the bird is and how it was handled is important, and I can always freeze the excess cuts myself. Store all poultry refrigerated, wrapped in food wrapping, and away from contact with other foods. If you stick to chicken because it's familiar, my last bit of advice is to try cooking other birds. In this chapter you'll find duck, Cornish hen, Guinea hen, and others. They're no more difficult to prepare than chicken, and the range of flavors they add to your repertoire will pay big dividends every time you work up the gumption to wing it with a new one.

CHICKEN BREASTS WITH CHIVE AND MUSTARD SAUCE

SERVES 4

ONE OF MY FAVORITE classic bistro dishes is steak Diane, a paragon of quick cooking that finds steak swathed in a cream sauce mightily seasoned with mustard and enhanced with cognac. The next time you find yourself feeling those bistro pangs, try my take on steak Diane, made with chicken instead of beef, and my version of the traditional sauce with shallots and mustard. Roasted Garlic Mashed Potatoes (page 237) is a perfect accompaniment; the potatoes will soak up the sauce. Or serve it with The Best Fries You've Ever Made! (page 238) and an ice-cold Belgian beer.

2 tablespoons unsalted butter

Four 8-ounce skinless, boneless chicken breasts, slightly pounded and flattened

Fine sea salt and freshly ground black pepper

3 tablespoons chopped shallots

½ cup brandy, apple brandy, pear brandy, or Kentucky bourbon

½ cup dry white wine

3 tablespoons Dijon mustard

1½ cups homemade chicken stock (page 69) or store-bought, low-sodium chicken broth

½ cup heavy cream

3 tablespoons minced fresh chives

1. Heat the butter in a wide, heavy-bottomed sauté pan until it begins to melt and foam. Season the chicken with salt and pepper. Add the breasts to the pan and brown them on one side, 6 to 8 minutes. Turn them over and cook them until well browned on the other side, about 6 more minutes. The chicken is done when it is firm to the touch and the juices run clear. Transfer the chicken to a plate and cover with foil to keep warm.

2. Add the shallots to the same pan and sauté until softened but not browned, about 2 minutes. Lower the heat, move the pan away from the flame, lean away from it, and carefully pour in the brandy, taking care not

INSTEAD OF CHICKEN, use small beefsteaks or pork loin chops. Cooking time will vary based on thickness and desired doneness, but will be about 2 minutes more per side than the chicken.

FOR A SPICIER SAUCE, add 1 teaspoon hot, dry, English mustard to the sauce along with the Dijon.

to let it flame. (If it does flame, cover with a pot lid until the brandy cooks out.) Continuing to be mindful of potential flare-ups, return the pan to the stove and let the brandy evaporate over low heat.

3.   Add the wine to the pan, raise the heat to high, and bring it to a boil. Whisk in the mustard and let reduce for 1 minute. Pour in the broth and cook for 2 to 3 minutes more.

4.   Stir in the cream and bring just to a boil. Stir in the chives. Return the chicken breasts to the pan and simmer gently until the stock has reduced and thickened slightly, 4 to 5 minutes.

5.   To serve, put 1 chicken breast in the center of each of 4 plates and spoon some sauce over the top.

BRAISED CHICKEN WITH BUTTERNUT SQUASH, WALNUTS, AND SAGE

SERVES 4

When fall comes around, I find myself eager to cook with seasonal ingredients. Squash, sage, and walnuts are high on my list of autumnal all-stars and, plain and simple, this is a recipe that calls on those ingredients in a dish that could be prepared very spontaneously when the first cold night arrives next year.

2 tablespoons olive oil or vegetable oil

3 tablespoons unsalted butter

One 3½-pound chicken, cut into 8 pieces (2 breasts, 2 wings, 2 legs, 2 thighs)

Fine sea salt and freshly ground black pepper

½ small onion, diced

1 carrot, diced

2 cups butternut squash, peeled and cut into 1-inch dice (about 2 pounds squash)

1 tablespoon ground cinnamon

½ teaspoon ground cloves

½ teaspoon ground ginger

1½ cups homemade chicken stock (page 69) or low-sodium, store-bought chicken broth, simmering in a pot

½ cup finely chopped walnuts, plus more for serving

2 tablespoons chopped sage, plus more for serving

1. Heat the oil and melt 1 tablespoon of the butter in a high-sided sauté pan over medium heat. Season the chicken parts generously with salt and pepper. Add the chicken pieces to the pan, skin side down, without crowding and cook slowly until golden brown, about 8 minutes. Turn the pieces over and brown the other side, about 8 more minutes.

2. Transfer the chicken pieces to a plate and cover loosely with foil to keep warm. Set aside.

3. Add the onion, carrot, and squash to the pan and sauté until softened but still holding their shape, 6 to 8 minutes. Stir in the cinnamon, cloves, and ginger. Pour in the hot stock, return the chicken to the pan, raise the

USE QUARTERED CORNISH HENS instead of chicken, cooking them until the juices run clear.

TRY THIS WITH DARK MEAT ONLY and serve a quick, uncooked fresh cranberry relish on the side. Make the relish by blending 1 cup fresh cranberries, ½ cup water, and 1 cup sugar to a chunky consistency in a food processor fitted with the steel blade. To turn the relish into a salsa, add some ancho chile powder and lime juice.

heat to high, and bring the liquid to a boil. Lower the heat and let simmer until the chicken shows no pink when pierced at the joint, about 20 minutes. Taste the sauce and season it with salt and pepper.

4.   Remove the chicken from the pan and arrange the pieces on a serving platter. Add the walnuts and sage leaves to the pan and cook for 2 minutes. Add the remaining 2 tablespoons butter, stirring it in to give the sauce a smooth finish.

5.   Spoon the vegetables around the chicken and pour any extra sauce over the chicken. Sprinkle more sage and walnuts over the dish and serve.

HERB-ROASTED CAPON

SERVES 6 TO 8

THERE'S NOTHING WRONG WITH ROASTED CHICKEN, but there is something particularly satisfying about a larger bird, like turkey, that can be served in thin slices rather than in sections like drumstick, thigh, and wing. When you're craving that kind of a meal, and a turkey is too large for your crowd, try a capon. Because of their high fat content in both white and dark meat, capons are moist and mildly flavored. And, because you don't see this bird every day, it's inherently special. Serve this with Savory Chipotle Chile Muffins (page 246) or Country Bread Stuffing with Onions and Sage (page 244).

One 7- to 8-pound capon

Coarse salt and freshly ground black pepper

4 garlic cloves, crushed

About 6 thyme sprigs

About 6 rosemary sprigs

1 medium onion, coarsely chopped

1 lemon, halved

3 tablespoons olive oil

1 cup homemade chicken stock (page 69) or low-sodium, store-bought chicken broth

3 tablespoons all-purpose flour

4 tablespoons (½ stick) unsalted butter

1. Preheat the oven to 425°F. Put a heavy-bottomed roasting pan in the oven for 5 minutes.

2. Season the capon cavity with salt and pepper, then stuff the cavity with the garlic, half the thyme, and half the rosemary. Put the onion and lemon halves in the cavity. Tie the capon together at the legs with kitchen twine to keep the bird's shape and help it cook evenly.

3. Rub the outside of the capon with the oil.

4. Put the capon in the roasting pan and roast for 45 minutes. Lower the oven temperature to 350°F and continue roasting for an additional 1 hour and 15 minutes. Chop the remaining herbs, stir together in a bowl, and sprinkle evenly over the capon. Roast for another 15 minutes, or until the

FILL THE CAPON'S CAVITY with more herbs and garlic to intensify the flavor. Halve 2 or 3 whole heads of garlic instead of the 4 cloves and stuff them into the cavity with the herbs. The garlic will mellow and infuse the capon with flavor during roasting.

juices run clear when the capon is pierced with a sharp, thin-bladed knife at the leg joint. If the juices are still pink, return the pan to the oven and perform the same test every 10 minutes until the juices run clear.

5. Remove the pan from the oven, transfer the capon to a carving board, and let rest for 15 to 20 minutes.

6. While the capon is resting, pour the broth into a pot and heat it over medium-high heat. At the same time, put the roasting pan on the stove over medium heat, skim off any remaining fat with a spoon, add the flour, and whisk it into the drippings. Whisk in the hot broth. Use a spoon to scrape up all the flavorful crusty bits cooked onto the bottom of the pan and bring the liquid to a boil. Cook until reduced and slightly thickened, about 5 minutes, then whisk in the butter. Remove the pan from the heat and strain the pan gravy into a sauceboat to pass at the table.

7. Carve the capon as you would a turkey: disjoint the legs and serve them whole, cut the thighs into 2 pieces; remove the breast from the breastbone; disjoint and remove the wings and serve them whole; and carve the breasts by cutting against the grain of the meat across the length of the breast.

8. Attractively arrange the meat on a platter and pass at the table with the sauce alongside in a sauceboat.

GUINEA HEN BREAST AND CHANTERELLES

SERVES 4

GUINEA HEN IS A DOMESTICATED BIRD with a flavor similar to pheasant but the hen doesn't dry out. Game birds are a creative alternative to chicken and this dish can be a starting point for your discovery of birds like pheasant and squab, most of which are either readily available in specialty meat markets or can be special-ordered by just about any butcher. Ask the butcher to French-cut the bone, leave the wing bone attached, and discard the breastbone, if the hen is not sold already cut this way.

I suggest you make the polenta first and keep it warm in a double boiler over simmering water.

1 cup slab bacon cut into ¼-inch cubes (about ½ pound bacon)

1 cup fresh pearl onions, blanched and peeled (defrosted frozen pearl onions can be substituted)

Olive oil, if necessary

Four 10-ounce guinea hen breasts

Fine sea salt and freshly ground black pepper

1 cup thinly sliced cremini mushrooms (about 6 ounces)

½ cup chanterelle mushrooms, cleaned of any debris and torn in half by hand

1 cup dry red wine

1 cup homemade chicken stock (page 69) or low-sodium, store-bought chicken broth

½ cup demi-glace (sold refrigerated or frozen in gourmet markets) or 1 cup low-sodium,

store-bought beef broth reduced by half and thickened with 2 tablespoons butter and 2 tablespoons all-purpose flour

3 tablespoons unsalted butter

2 tablespoons thyme

2 tablespoons marjoram or oregano

Soft Herbed Polenta (page 113)

1. Preheat the oven to 350°F.

2. Heat a sauté pan over medium heat. Put in the bacon cubes and cook until evenly browned and most of the fat has been rendered, about 10 minutes. Use tongs or a slotted spoon to transfer the bacon to a paper towel–lined plate to drain, leaving the fat in the pan.

USE CORNISH HEN or poussin instead of the guinea hen.

SINCE CHANTERELLES ARE HARD TO FIND and expensive, substitute a 2-ounce package of dried chanterelles, rehydrated in hot water for 20 minutes, drained, and added along with the cremini mushrooms.

3. Put the pearl onions in the pan and sauté until they begin to caramelize, about 3 minutes, taking care not to let them burn. Lower the heat and continue to sauté until they begin to soften, 4 to 5 minutes. Use tongs or a slotted spoon to transfer the onions to a bowl and set them aside, leaving any remaining bacon fat in the pan.

4. If there is not enough fat remaining in the pan to generously coat the bottom, pour in some olive oil and let it heat up. Season the guinea hen breasts with salt and pepper and put them in the pan. Cook over medium heat until brown on both sides, about 8 minutes per side. Remove the breasts from the pan, transfer to a small roasting pan, and roast until thoroughly cooked and firm to the touch, 8 to 10 minutes. Remove from the pan and cover with foil to keep warm.

5. Meanwhile, make the sauce. Pour off any excess fat from the sauté pan and add the cremini and chanterelle mushrooms. Cook until golden and slightly wilted, 3 to 4 minutes, return the onions and bacon to the pan, and sauté briefly to combine the flavors. Pour in the wine and let reduce for 1 minute.

6. Pour the chicken stock and demi-glace into the pan and bring it to a boil over high heat. Reduce the heat until the liquid is simmering. Add the breasts to the sauce and braise until the liquid has reduced by half and the breasts are fully cooked—when pierced with a knife, the juices should run clear, about 5 minutes. Add the butter to the sauce and swirl or gently whisk to combine. Stir in the thyme and marjoram.

7. To serve, mound some polenta on each of 4 dinner plates and rest a guinea hen breast on top. Spoon some sauce over the hen and serve.

ROASTED CORNISH HEN WITH AN HERB CRUST

MAKES 2 WHOLE HEN OR 4 HALF HEN SERVINGS

ONE OF THE GREAT BENEFITS of Cornish hens is their size; one hen can be a portion in itself, or split to make two portions. This recipe, which does just enough to the hens to punch up their flavor, can easily be multiplied to serve as many people as you like. Serve this with Curried Pea Soup with Frizzled Ginger (page 63).

8 tablespoons (1 stick) unsalted butter

1 egg yolk

1 cup dried breadcrumbs

2 tablespoons chopped rosemary

¼ cup chopped flat-leaf parsley

⅓ cup Dijon mustard

1 tablespoon mustard seeds

Two 1½-pound Cornish hens, split down the back, backbone removed, and butterflied

Fine sea salt and freshly ground black pepper

2 tablespoons olive oil

1. Well in advance (½ hour to 1 week) of making the hens, put the butter, egg yolk, breadcrumbs, rosemary, parsley, and Dijon mustard in a food processor fitted with the steel blade and pulse until thoroughly mixed. Scrape the mixture into a bowl and fold in the mustard seeds. Set aside if you will continue within half an hour or cover and refrigerate for up to 1 week; let come to room temperature before proceeding.

2. Preheat the oven to 350°F.

3. Season the hens with salt and pepper. Heat the oil in a heavy-bottomed sauté pan over medium heat for 2 minutes. Put the Cornish hens, breast and skin side down, in the pan, and cook to a crispy, light golden brown, about 5 minutes. Turn them over and cook for 5 minutes more on the butterflied, inside-bone side. Remove the hens from the sauté pan and let cool for several minutes.

MAKE THIS WITH YOUNG,
1-POUND SPRING CHICKENS
(called poussins) or boneless
breasts of chickens, cooking them
until the juices run clear.

VARY THE HERBS, making this
with thyme, sage, oregano, or
a combination.

4. Spread a generous coating of herb and mustard butter on the breast side of the hens.

5. Put the hens in a roasting pan and roast until the juices run clear and the Cornish hens' internal temperature reads 165°F on an instant-read thermometer, 20 to 25 minutes. If the herb and mustard coating darkens too quickly, tent the hens with aluminum foil for the remainder of the cooking time.

6. Remove the hens from the oven and allow to cool for 5 minutes before serving.

PAN-ROASTED QUAIL WITH FIGS AND PORT

SERVES 4

Because of their small size, quail, farm raised and widely available, make an outstanding appetizer or main course. The meat is somewhat dark but not unpleasantly gamey, as you might expect. In fact, it's surprisingly mild in flavor, almost earthy, thanks to the birds' diet. This is one of those recipes that's special because it's so classic; the sweet port wine lends it a timeless appeal and elegance.

3 tablespoons olive oil

2 medium carrots, peeled and roughly chopped (about ½ cup)

1 medium onion, cut into medium dice (about ½ cup)

3 celery stalks, roughly chopped (about ¾ cup)

1 bay leaf

½ teaspoon chopped thyme plus 4 large thyme sprigs

1 garlic clove, smashed

½ cup demi-glace (sold refrigerated or frozen in gourmet markets), or 1 cup low-sodium, store-bought beef broth reduced by half and thickened with 2 tablespoons butter and 2 tablespoons all-purpose flour combined

1½ cups homemade chicken stock (page 69) or low-sodium, store-bought chicken or beef broth

½ cup plus 2 tablespoons high-quality port

Eight 4-ounce quail (sold fresh and partially boned, 4 to a package)

Fine sea salt and freshly ground black pepper

12 fresh figs, halved (8 to 10 halved, dried white figs can be substituted)

2 tablespoons unsalted butter

¼ cup pine nuts or pumpkin seeds

1. Set a 3-quart saucepan over medium heat to warm it. Pour in 2 table-spoons of the oil and heat for 2 minutes. Add the carrots, onion, celery, bay leaf, chopped thyme, and garlic to the pan and pan-roast, turning occasionally, until everything is well browned, about 12 minutes. Pour in the demi-glace and broth, return to a boil, then lower the heat and let sim-mer until reduced by half, about 30 minutes.

2. Pour the port into the pot and simmer for 10 minutes. Strain the sauce through a fine-mesh strainer set over a bowl. The sauce can be made up

INSTEAD OF QUAIL, use fresh, uncooked turkey breast, cut into 4-ounce cutlets, cooked like the quail and served in the same manner.

THE PORT SAUCE can be used to top any number of meats, including chicken, beef, or pork.

to this point, cooled, covered, and refrigerated for up to 2 days. Reheat gently over medium heat before cooking the quail.

3. Preheat the oven to 325°F.

4. Season the quail inside and out with salt and pepper. If there is a metal frame inside the quail (often included by the purveyor to hold the shape while cooking), leave it in and remove it before serving.

5. Pour the remaining 1 tablespoon oil into a large, heavy-bottomed sauté pan and heat it over medium heat for 1 minute. Add the thyme sprigs and quail, breast side down. Cook the quail until dark golden brown, about 3 minutes, then turn them over and cook the back until well browned, about 4 more minutes.

6. Remove the quail from the skillet, set them on a cookie sheet, and keep them warm in the oven while you finish the dish.

7. Add the figs to the pan in which the quail were cooked and roast over medium-high heat for 1 minute. Use tongs to pick out and discard the thyme sprigs. Add the warm port sauce to the figs and whisk the butter into the sauce to enrich it and give it a silken sheen.

8. Divide the quail among 4 dinner plates, top each serving with figs, and spoon some port sauce over the top. Scatter some pine nuts over each quail and serve.

BLACK CURRANT–LACQUERED DUCK BREAST

SERVES 4

THIS DISH IS MUCH SIMPLER than it reads or looks. The duck is pan-roasted on the stovetop and the lacquer comes together quickly in the same pan. The combination takes its cue from the hoisin sauce that's traditionally served with Peking duck to balance the rich, crisp-skinned bird with sweet relief. Serve this with Quinoa "Risotto" with Toasted Hazelnuts and Dried Currants (page 106) or Curried Wheat Berries with Sweet Onions (page 108).

Four 6- to 8-ounce whole duck breasts, or two 1-pound magret duck breasts (from a Moulard duck)

Fine sea salt and freshly ground black pepper

3 tablespoons chopped shallots

1 tablespoon grated ginger

2 tablespoons honey

½ cup black currant jam

¼ cup cider vinegar

1. Preheat the oven to 375°F.

2. With the point of a knife, score the skin side of the duck breasts in a crosshatch pattern, being careful not to pierce the flesh. This helps release and render the layer of fat under the skin and makes the finished duck look stunning.

3. Heat a sauté pan over medium heat for 2 minutes. Season the duck breasts with salt and pepper. Put the breasts in the pan, skin side down, and cook over medium to low heat to render the fat and brown the skin, 6 to 8 minutes. Carefully drain off and discard any accumulated fat from the pan and return the pan to the stove.

4. Carefully turn the breasts over and brown the flesh side for 3 to 4 minutes, or several more minutes for magret breasts. Remove the breasts to a plate and cover to keep warm.

SEMI-BONELESS QUAIL can be cooked following the same recipe and cooking times.

IN THE SUMMER, grill chicken breasts with the skin on, basting with the lacquer as they cook.

5.   Add the shallots to the pan and return the pan to the heat. Sauté the shallots until softened but not browned, 2 minutes, then add the ginger, honey, jam, and vinegar and stir. Bring to a simmer and let simmer for 2 or 3 minutes to reduce and thicken to a lacquer-like glaze.

6.   Put the breasts, skin side up, on a nonstick cookie sheet, brush some lacquer on the upward-facing side of each breast, and reheat in the oven for 3 minutes.

7.   To serve, slice the breasts lengthwise or crosswise and arrange the slices of 1 breast on each of 4 plates. Quickly reheat the sauce, if necessary, and drizzle some around the duck breasts.

ROASTED LONG ISLAND DUCKLING WITH RHUBARB COMPOTE

SERVES 4

Every spring, long stalks of rhubarb turn up for a few precious weeks. This tart fruit is usually cooked in simple desserts like cobblers and pies, but the sweet-and-sour rhubarb syrup here takes a savory turn as a complement to rich duck.

One 7-pound Long Island or Peking-style duckling

Fine sea salt and freshly ground black pepper

3 bay leaves

4 thyme sprigs

4 rosemary sprigs

½ cup cider vinegar

½ cup dry white wine

¾ cup sugar

3 coin-size slices peeled ginger

1½ teaspoons ground cinnamon

1 tablespoon freshly squeezed lemon juice

1 pound rhubarb, all green leaves discarded, peeled and cut crosswise into ¼-inch-thick pieces

1. Preheat the oven to 375°F. Put a roasting pan in the oven.

2. Season the duck inside and out with salt and pepper. Put the bay leaves inside the duck, along with the thyme and rosemary sprigs. Pierce the skin of the duck repeatedly, front and back, with the tines of a fork. This will allow the fat to drain away, leaving a crisp, golden skin.

3. Put the duck, breast side down, directly into the roasting pan. Roast until it begins to brown, about 25 minutes, periodically and very carefully pouring the fat at the bottom of the pan into a heatproof container.

4. Use tongs or a meat fork to turn the duck onto its back. Brush the duck with some of the cider vinegar, being careful to avoid splattering. Continue to roast the duck for another 1½ hours, pouring off the fat and basting it with cider vinegar every 15 minutes to help keep the meat moist and produce a crisp, golden skin while rendering most of the fat.

PEACHES, PLUMS, AND APRI-COTS are all classic combinations with duck. Make this same recipe, using any of those fruits in the syrupy compote. Allow a bit more time for firmer fruits to cook until tender but not mushy.

5. While the duck is roasting, make the rhubarb compote: Put the wine, sugar, ginger, cinnamon, lemon juice, and ¼ cup water in a saucepot large enough to hold the rhubarb. Bring to a boil over high heat, then lower the heat and let simmer for 5 minutes to cook the sugar syrup. Add the rhubarb pieces and cook for 5 minutes more to coat them with the hot syrup. Remove the pan from the heat and let cool.

6. When the duck is fully cooked, remove it from the oven and allow to rest for 15 minutes before placing on a platter or a cutting board and carving it: use a sharp knife to separate the breast from the breast bone, sliding the knife down along the keel bone of the breast bone, angling the knife along the bone to separate the breast from the bone. Slide the knife tip through the wing joint that joins the breast and discard the wing completely. Slice off the leg from the carcass and separate the joint of the leg and thigh. Remove the thigh from the carcass by cutting through the joint at the backbone. Discard the carcass. Slice the breast meat into thin slices, and separate the leg and thigh.

7. Serve the duck with some of the rhubarb compote spooned over the top.

PRIME RIBS AND

Meat and Game

FINAL CUTS

hether for a special occasion or a weeknight family meal, meats and game lend an air of celebration to any dinner. Meat is a special treat, something that we all crave.

On the more casual side, this chapter includes crowd-pleasers like Skillet-Charred Pepper-Crusted Burger, My Mother's Italian-American Meatloaf, and Texas-Style Oven-Barbecued Beef Brisket. At the other end of the spectrum are a number of dishes perfect for any get together, including holiday feasts. These include Standing Rib of Beef and Turkish Braised Lamb Shanks with Roasted Plums.

In between these two extremes are fun, big-flavored dishes suitable for everything from an afternoon pool party to a Saturday night dinner party, such as Boneless Roast Leg of Lamb with Feta, Olives, and Eggplant; Charred Beef Medallions with Poblano-Tequila Sauce; and Barbecued Spare Ribs and Mango Barbecue Jam.

Many of the recipes in this chapter yield up to 8 servings, which I hope anticipates your serving them to a large group, or you can plan on leftovers to enjoy the next day.

TEXAS-STYLE OVEN-BARBECUED BEEF BRISKET

SERVES 6 TO 8

BEEF BRISKET IS ONE OF THE CLASSICS of American home cooking. Well, as I've said before in this book, anything can be made special if you take a fresh look at it. In the case of brisket, the fact that it requires slow cooking can be a cue to apply other slow-cooking conventions to it. One of my favorites is Texas-style barbecue, in which a salt and pepper dry rub is applied to the meat before it's cooked for hours in a smoker. Here, we make it right in the oven. Accompaniments are virtually unlimited, but some of my favorites are Roasted Garlic Mashed Potatoes (page 237), Savory Chipotle Chile Muffins (page 246), and Glazed Whole-Roasted Shallots (page 251).

2 tablespoons ground cumin

2 tablespoons ground coriander

4 garlic cloves, minced

½ cup light brown sugar

1½ teaspoons cayenne pepper

Fine sea salt and coarsely ground (butcher grind) black pepper

One 4- to 5-pound beef brisket, deckle (fattier) end if available

Hot sauce, Tabasco, and/or barbecue sauce, for serving

1. Preheat the oven to 325°F.

2. Put the cumin, coriander, garlic, sugar, cayenne, ¼ cup salt, and ¼ cup pepper in a bowl and stir them together. Rub the seasoning mix all over the beef, really working it into the meat. Put the meat on a plate or platter, cover loosely with plastic wrap, and refrigerate overnight. Let come to room temperature before proceeding.

3. Put a rack in a roasting pan and pour ½ inch water into the bottom of the pan to catch the drippings and keep the beef from drying out. Put the beef on the rack in the oven and slow-cook for 2 hours, adding additional

TO MAKE A POT ROAST BARBE-
CUE BRISKET, add 2 cups water
and leave out the rack, cooking the
meat directly in the roasting pan.

water, if necessary, to keep the bottom of the pan wet and prevent the drippings from burning. Use tongs or a meat fork to turn the beef over, cover the pan with a tight-fitting lid or aluminum foil, and cook for another 1½ to 2 hours. During this time, much of the fat will render into the water.

4. Transfer the brisket to a platter, cover with foil, and let rest for 20 to 30 minutes before carving crosswise against the grain into ½-inch-thick slices.

5. Arrange the slices on a platter and serve with hot sauce, Tabasco, and/or barbecue sauce.

STANDING RIB OF BEEF

SERVES 6 TO 8

Usually, I think of a special as something spontaneous, but it can also be planned weeks in advance and served at just the right moment. A rib of beef is a special dinner for a special occasion. While this looks very impressive, it is virtually foolproof. Perhaps best of all, any leftovers can be used for Roast Beef and Mushroom Hash (page 210).

One 4½- to 5-pound oven-ready rib roast of beef (4 or 5 rib bones)

¼ cup olive oil

¼ cup coarsely ground black pepper

3 tablespoons fine sea salt

2 tablespoons chopped garlic

3 tablespoons chopped thyme

3 tablespoons chopped rosemary

YOUR NIGHTLY SPECIALS

EXPERIMENT WITH THE HERB AND SEASONING CRUST, adding spices like those in Texas-Style Oven-Barbecued Beef Brisket (page 200) or rubbing the rib roast with barbecue dry rub spices like paprika, cumin, and chili powder.

1. Preheat the oven to 425°F.

2. Brush the meat with the oil. Combine all of the seasonings in a small bowl. Rub the seasoning paste uniformly over the meat. Put the meat, bone side down, in a roasting pan and roast for 20 minutes.

3. Lower the oven temperature to 350°F and continue roasting until an instant-read thermometer inserted near the center of the roast reads 130°F for medium-rare, 1½ to 2 hours. Periodically and very carefully pour the fat that has accumulated in the roasting pan into a heatproof container.

4. Remove the roast from the oven and let stand for 20 minutes before carving.

5. After the roast has rested for 20 minutes, carefully transfer it bone side down to a large cutting board. Insert a sharp knife between the meat and the rib bones, separating the meat from the ribs in 1 large piece. Carve the boneless meat into ½-inch-thick slices. Cut between the rib bones, separating them into individual bones, and serve as a bonus on the side.

MUSTARD-GLAZED BEEF SHORT RIBS

SERVES 4 TO 6

W**ITH SLOW,** moist braising, short ribs turn succulent, tender, and intensely beefy. Here, the ribs are braised, then roasted, to bring out even more flavor. The braising can take place one, two, or even three days before the final grilling. To me, that's a cue to double the recipe and have enough ribs on tap for a second meal later in the week.

¼ cup olive oil

6 pounds beef short ribs, on the bone, cut into 4 portions

Fine sea salt and freshly ground black pepper

1 large onion, chopped

2 carrots, peeled and chopped

1 celery stalk, chopped

1 jalapeño pepper, seeded and chopped, optional

2 garlic cloves, crushed

¼ cup tomato paste

1 cup red wine

3 cups low-sodium, store-bought beef broth

Bouquet garni: 3 rosemary sprigs, 3 thyme sprigs, and 3 oregano sprigs, tied in a cheesecloth

½ cup Pommery mustard

½ cup honey

1. Preheat the oven to 350°F.

2. Pour the oil into a wide, deep-sided sauté pan and heat it over medium-high heat. Season the short ribs with salt and pepper, add them to the pan, and brown them all over, about 4 minutes per side. Transfer the ribs to a large casserole or roasting pan.

3. Add the onion, carrots, and celery to the sauté pan and cook for 5 minutes to lightly caramelize them. Add the jalapeño, garlic, tomato paste, wine, and broth to the pan. Bring the mixture to a rapid boil, then pour it over the ribs in the casserole. The liquid should not rise more than two-thirds up the side of the ribs and the ribs should not be entirely submerged. If you have extra liquid, maybe your casserole is too small and the ribs are too tightly packed; try dividing the ribs and liquid among two casseroles.

ALMOST ANY FLAVOR can be introduced into the braising liquid. Add cumin and cilantro or leave out the Southwestern ingredients in favor of Asian spice notes with ½ cup soy sauce in place of the wine and several slices of fresh ginger and even star anise if you have it. Or replace the wine with dark beer and see how that turns it richer and earthy flavored.

4. Put the casserole in the oven, add the bouquet garni, and braise the ribs for about 1½ hours. Pierce the ribs with the tines of a fork, if cooked enough, the fork will meet no resistance.

5. Remove the casserole from the oven and let rest for 5 to 10 minutes before transferring the ribs to a plate or platter. Degrease the braising liquid, strain it, discard the solids, and reduce and reserve the juices for serving. The short ribs can be cooled, covered, and refrigerated for 1 to 3 days. Let come to room temperature before proceeding.

6. Prepare an outdoor grill with a drip pan to prevent flare-ups or preheat the oven to 350°F.

7. Combine the mustard and honey in a bowl and liberally brush over the ribs. Grill or cook the ribs in the oven for 10 minutes, turning once, until the glaze is caramelized, dark, and delicious. If grilling, brush on more glaze as the ribs cook.

8. Serve the ribs family style, passing the reduced braising liquid alongside in a sauceboat.

CHARRED BEEF MEDALLIONS WITH POBLANO-TEQUILA SAUCE

SERVES 4

TRY THIS IN YOUR KITCHEN and you may find yourself ready to take a plunge into deeper Southwestern waters. It's an uncomplicated recipe that uses fairly familiar ingredients (e.g., tequila, lime juice, Grand Marnier) to conjure up a little margarita-fueled fun. You might not have used a poblano chile before but—trust me—it's just as easy to seed and chop as a bell pepper. (It's a fresh chile that runs the gamut from no-detectable-heat to mildly spicy.)

This recipe also uses filet mignon, a popular cut of meat (it's a medallion cut from the tenderloin), in a Southwestern context. Pan sauces are a user-friendly way to make a quick and satisfying dinner of filet mignon. Traditionally, they use red wine, cognac, or Madeira. As good as those are, I find that the qualities of a filet—which isn't as beefy as, say, a sirloin—are perfectly suited to the chile and citrus accents of Southwestern cooking, so I have used margarita-friendly tequila here.

1½ pounds filet mignon, cut into four 1-inch-thick medallions

Fine sea salt and freshly ground black pepper

2 tablespoons olive oil

2 tablespoons unsalted butter

1 small Vidalia onion or other sweet onion, cut into medium dice

1 poblano chile, seeded and cut into julienne

1 tablespoon ground cumin

¼ cup gold tequila (the higher the quality, the better the flavor in the finished dish)

¼ cup freshly squeezed lime juice

1 cup low-sodium, store-bought beef broth

¼ cup orange liqueur, such as Grand Marnier

¼ cup honey

1 tablespoon grated orange zest

½ cup sour cream

NIGHTLY SPECIALS

IF YOU ADORE SPICY, SMOKY FOOD, turn up the heat by replacing the poblano with a roughly chopped chipotle pepper in adobo sauce. You can also use a seeded, minced jalapeño chile. For a less spicy dish, use a red bell pepper.

THE BEEF CAN EASILY BE REPLACED BY CHICKEN CUTLETS (increase cooking time to about 5 minutes per side) or medium peeled shrimp (reduce cooking time to a total of 4 to 5 minutes in the pan).

YOU CAN EXPAND THE DISH by garnishing it with sunflower seeds, pine nuts, or sliced almonds and/or by adding a total of ½ cup diced tomato and/or zucchini to the pan at the end of step 5, just before seasoning with salt and pepper.

FOR A SOPHISTICATED SOFT TACO, refrigerate any leftover filet mignon. Roughly chop it, quickly warm it in a pan with just a little olive oil, then divide among flour tortillas. Top with queso blanco, shredded lettuce, diced plum tomatoes, and your favorite salsa.

1. Warm a deep-sided sauté pan over medium-high heat, letting it get very hot. Season the beef medallions all over with salt and pepper. Add the olive oil and butter to the pan. When the butter has melted, add the beef medallions to the pan without crowding. Raise the heat to high and char both sides of the beef well, 3 to 4 minutes per side. For rare to medium-rare beef, cook quickly, turning once only after the beef has browned on the first side. (For well-done meat, transfer the beef to a cookie sheet and place in an oven preheated to 300°F while you make the sauce.)

2. Remove the beef from the pan, place on a warm platter, cover with foil, and set aside. Do not discard the pan juices and fat.

3. Add the onion and poblano to the sauté pan, spread them out in a single, even layer, and cook until wilted, about 4 minutes. Add the cumin and stir to toast the spice.

4. Working carefully away from the flame, add the tequila to the pan and deglaze by swirling the tequila. Set the pan over low heat until the liquid has reduced to almost dry.

5. Add the lime juice and reduce to almost dry. Add the broth, raise the heat to high, and reduce the liquid by half. Add the orange liqueur, honey, and orange zest. Cook for 2 minutes and then add the sour cream. Do not allow to boil, but gently simmer for 2 minutes. Season to taste with salt and pepper.

6. Spoon some sauce onto each of 4 dinner plates. Place a medallion in the center of each plate, spoon some sauce over the top, and serve.

KENTUCKY BOURBON SIRLOIN STEAK

SERVES 4

Harmony is achieved in a dish when contrasting flavors combine to create balance. In this dish, the black pepper and bourbon add a real jolt of flavor that's miraculously mellowed by the cream and butter.

3 tablespoons coarsely ground black peppercorns

Four 10-ounce New York–cut sirloin steaks, also called shell steaks

Fine sea salt

2 tablespoons olive oil

¼ cup finely chopped shallots

⅓ cup Kentucky bourbon

1 cup low-sodium store-bought beef broth

½ cup heavy cream

2 tablespoons unsalted butter

YOUR NIGHTLY SPECIALS

USE VEAL CHOPS, pork chops, or beef rib steaks instead of sirloin. Cook in the same fashion but allow a longer cooking time, about 8 minutes per side for a 1-inch-thick chop or rib steak with the bone intact.

REPLACE THE BOURBON with brandy or cognac.

FOR A LIGHTER PAN SAUCE, leave out the cream and butter.

1. Put the black peppercorns in a wide, flat dish. Press the steaks into the peppers to coat them on all sides, then season with salt. Set aside.

2. Heat the oil in a large, heavy-bottomed sauté pan over high heat for 1 minute. Add the steaks, two at a time if necessary to avoid overcrowding, and cook for 3 minutes per side for medium-rare. Transfer each steak to a dinner plate and set aside.

3. Add the shallots to the pan and cook for 2 minutes over medium heat. Remove the pan from the heat and add the bourbon, then carefully return the pan to the stove over low heat and cook until the bourbon is almost entirely evaporated, about 2 minutes. Pour in the broth, raise the heat to high, bring it to a boil, and continue to boil until reduced and thickened, 3 to 5 minutes. Swirl in the cream and the butter and warm gently.

4. Pour some sauce over each steak and serve.

ROAST BEEF AND MUSHROOM HASH

SERVES 4 TO 6

PLANNED LEFTOVERS ARE EVEN MORE SPECIAL when they are transformed into a new dish as they are here, or turned into a hash or an assortment of uniformly cut and diced ingredients, usually well seasoned and quick to prepare. This can be made from scratch and is certainly worth the effort, and it's especially satisfying when made with the remains of a dish like Standing Rib of Beef (page 202).

2 russet potatoes (about 1½ pounds total), peeled, diced, and kept in cold water

¼ cup olive oil

1 large Spanish onion, diced

½ pound shiitake mushroom caps, or other exotic mushroom caps, sliced into julienne

Fine sea salt and freshly ground black pepper

2 pounds sirloin of beef, cut into ½-inch cubes

1 tablespoon chili powder

½ cup seeded plum tomato, cut into small dice

2 tablespoons chopped cilantro

1. Cover the potatoes with cold water in a heavy-bottomed pot, set over medium heat and bring to a boil. Lower the heat and cook the potatoes at a simmer until softened but still firm (it should still take a bit of force to push a knife tip into the center), about 12 minutes. Drain the potatoes and spread them out on a cookie sheet to cool them quickly.

2. Heat the oil in a wide, heavy-bottomed sauté pan over medium-high heat. Add the onion and sauté until golden, about 6 minutes. Add the potatoes and cook until they begin to brown, 4 to 5 minutes. Add the mushrooms and sauté until they begin to give off their liquid, 3 to 4 minutes more. Season the vegetables with 1 teaspoon salt and 1 teaspoon pepper, transfer to a bowl using a slotted spoon, and add the cubed beef to the hot oil in an even layer. Brown the beef over high heat, turning only

USE GRILLED CHICKEN BREAST or roast capon instead of beef.

THE TOMATOES can be replaced by blanched, halved baby beets.

when one side has browned, and browning all sides evenly and quickly to maintain a medium-rare interior, 7 to 8 minutes total. Season the beef with salt and pepper.

3.   Add the chili powder, diced tomato, and cilantro to the pan and return the cooked vegetables to the pan. Press down along the edges and cook over low heat so that a crust forms along the bottom. Turn the hash out onto a plate and serve family style from the center of the table.

MY MOTHER'S ITALIAN-AMERICAN MEATLOAF

SERVES 6

W E ALL HAVE MEMORIES *either of great or terrible meatloaf meals from childhood. My mom's meatloaf is a fond food memory. It was always moist and juicy, with a touch of Italy from the tomatoes and pecorino Romano cheese. It also passed the test of any respectable meatloaf: it made good sandwiches the next day.*

1 pound ground beef

1 pound ground veal

1 pound ground pork

1 cup milk

1 cup bread cubes (3 or 4 slices Italian country bread, crusts removed)

½ cup finely grated pecorino Romano

2 tablespoons minced garlic

1 onion, cut into small dice

2 eggs

2 tablespoons dried oregano

½ cup chopped flatleaf parsley

Fine sea salt and freshly ground black pepper

Olive oil, for greasing

1 cup canned plum tomatoes, crushed

2 tablespoons tomato paste

1 medium carrot, diced

1 stalk celery, diced

1. Preheat the oven to 350°F.

2. Put the beef, veal, and pork in a bowl and knead them together.

3. Pour the milk into a bowl and soak the bread in it, squeezing it into a paste. Add the soaked bread to the bowl with the meat and work them together as though you were kneading dough. Add the cheese, garlic, onion, eggs, oregano, and parsley. Season with salt and pepper and knead again until well incorporated.

4. Oil a large roasting pan with the olive oil. Form the meat mixture into a large loaf in the center of the roasting pan.

YOU CAN MAKE THE LOAF
WITH BEEF AND VEAL ONLY,
or with just beef.

LAY SOME RAW BACON STRIPS
OVER THE LOAF before baking.
(This was one way my mother
made her meatloaf extra special.)

ADD SOME SAUTÉED MUSH-
ROOMS to the pan during the last
20 minutes of cooking.

5. Stir the plum tomatoes, tomato paste, and 1 cup water together in a bowl and pour the mixture evenly over the meatloaf. Scatter the carrots and celery in the pan around the loaf.

6. Put the pan in the oven and bake until a skewer inserted in the center of the loaf comes out warm, about 1½ hours. If the loaf begins to look dry while cooking, tent it with aluminum foil. Remove the pan from the oven and let the meatloaf cool slightly.

7. Slice the meatloaf into servings, put 1 serving on each plate, and spoon pan gravy and vegetables over and around the meatloaf.

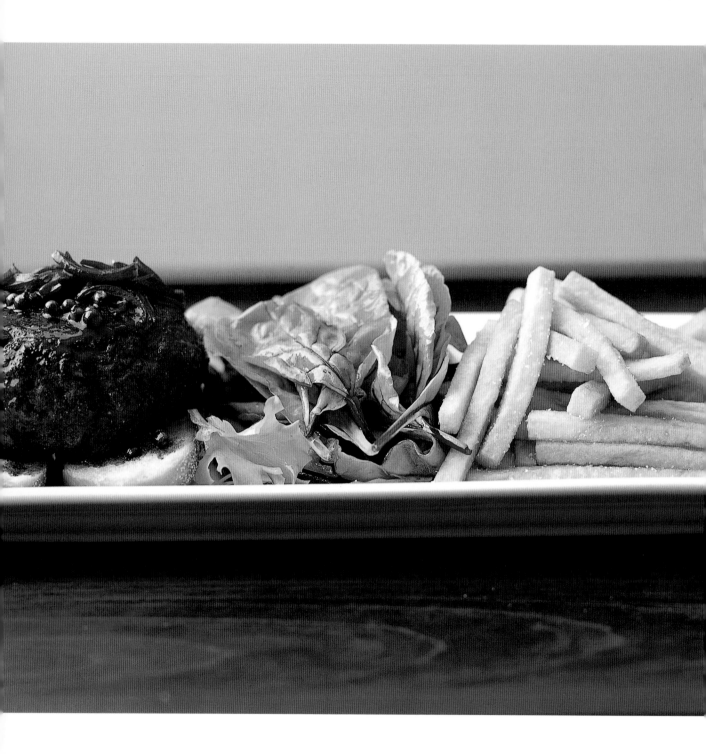

SKILLET-CHARRED PEPPER-CRUSTED BURGER

SERVES 4

W<small>HEN I WAS CHEF AT</small> '21', I gained a lifetime of burger-making experience. The '21' burger had to be great: it was once famously priced at $21, making it the restaurant's namesake offering. This recipe is based on the one I served at '21'. It isn't so much a burger as it is a chopped steak shaped into burger form. I prefer ground chuck and sirloin because they have a good fat content and lots of flavor. The key to this burger—which is meant to be eaten with knife and fork—is to go against bad habits and don't press down with the spatula at all. This will keep the burger juicy and full of natural flavor. The green peppercorn topping, though referred to as a sauce in the recipe, is more of a condiment, consisting only of peppercorns cooked in red wine and finished with butter. Serve this with a simple green salad and The Best Fries You've Ever Made! (page 238).

8 slices baguette, toasted

1 pound ground sirloin

1 pound ground chuck

Fine sea salt and freshly ground black pepper

¼ cup olive oil

4 large shallots, thinly sliced

2 tablespoons green peppercorns packed in brine, drained and crushed with the side of a wide-bladed knife

½ cup dry red wine, preferably Syrah or Zinfandel

4 tablespoons (½ stick) unsalted butter, cut into pieces

1. Push 2 baguette slices together in the center of each of 4 plates and set aside.

2. Combine the sirloin and chuck in a bowl and knead together briefly by hand. Form the meat into 4 burger patties, making them tight but not overly crushed together. Season each burger with salt and pepper.

GROUND LAMB OR TURKEY are both good burger meats. Be sure to cook the turkey sufficiently.

3.   Set a grill pan, or wide sauté pan, over medium-high heat and let it get nice and hot. Pour in 2 tablespoons of the oil and heat it for 1 minute. Add the burgers to the pan and char the burgers on both sides, about 4 minutes per side for medium-rare, 1 or 2 minutes less for rare, or 1 or 2 minutes well-done.

4.   Use a spatula to put 1 burger on the baguette slices on each plate and set aside.

5.   Pour the remaining 2 tablespoons oil into the pan, add the shallots, and sauté until they begin to crisp, taking care not to burn them. Add the peppercorns and sauté for 1 minute. Pour in the wine, raise the heat to high, bring to a boil, and continue to boil until reduced by half, about 3 minutes.

6.   Remove the pan from the heat and swirl the butter into the sauce, 1 piece at a time, then pour some sauce over each burger and serve.

GRILLED PORK CHOPS WITH COFFEE BARBECUE SAUCE

SERVES 4

B ECAUSE PORK CHOPS HAVE a tendency to dry out, especially over the extreme heat of a grill, I quick-brine them first to tenderize the meat and lock moisture in so when they're grilled, you have more margin for accurate cooking. Brining before grilling is not as spontaneous as other grilling, but once you've tried it, you'll never grill an unbrined pork chop again.

Fine sea salt and freshly ground black pepper

2 pounds pork chops, preferably center cut, ½ inch think

Coffee Barbecue Sauce (recipe follows)

NIGHTLY SPECIALS

CHICKEN BRINES BEAUTIFULLY as well, so make this recipe with chicken pieces. Or skip the brining and use the sauce to top grilled steak.

1. Pour 1 quart water into a deep container. Add ¼ cup salt and stir until it's dissolved.

2. Submerge the pork chops in the solution completely and weight them down with a plate if necessary. Refrigerate for at least 12 and no more than 24 hours.

3. Remove the chops from the brine and pat dry with paper towels.

4. Prepare an outdoor grill or preheat a grill pan over high heat on the stovetop.

5. Season the chops with salt and pepper and put them on the grill over direct heat. Cook for 5 minutes on each side, or less if the chops are thinly cut.

6. After turning the chops, baste them with the barbecue sauce, letting the sauce caramelize onto the pork.

7. Serve from a platter with extra barbecue sauce alongside.

COFFEE BARBECUE SAUCE

MAKES 1½ CUPS

½ cup brewed espresso or strong, dark coffee

1 cup ketchup

½ cup cider vinegar

½ cup firmly packed light brown sugar

1 onion, finely chopped (about 1 cup)

2 garlic cloves, crushed

3 fresh hot chiles, such as jalapeño, or hotter if desired, seeded

2 tablespoons hot dry mustard mixed with 1 tablespoon warm water

2 tablespoons Worcestershire sauce

2 tablespoons ground cumin

2 tablespoons chili powder

1. Stir all of the ingredients together in a small pot and bring to a simmer over medium-high heat. Lower the heat so the mixture is just simmering and let simmer for 20 minutes. Remove the pot from the heat, let the mixture cool, then puree it in a blender or food processor fitted with the steel blade.

2. The barbecue sauce can be covered and refrigerated for up to 2 weeks.

GARLIC AND RUM PORK ROAST

SERVES 6 TO 8

THIS PORK ROAST BEGAN FOR ME as a home-cooked special. Having just returned from Miami, I wanted to roast pork in the Cuban style and I wanted left-overs, too, for next-day Cuban sandwiches. Here's the recipe I came up with; it serves six and leaves enough to make sandwiches. Need I say it? Serve this with Cuban-Style Black Bean Soup (page 73), white rice, and Garlic-Roasted Yuca (page 242).

6 large garlic cloves

2 small white onions, coarsely chopped

1 small bunch flat-leaf parsley, bottom stems discarded (about ½ cup loosely packed)

Fine sea salt and freshly ground black pepper

¼ cup dark rum

½ cup light brown sugar

¼ cup freshly squeezed lime juice

¼ cup olive oil

One 4- to 5-pound fresh pork shoulder, trimmed of any excess fat, boned and tied (sometimes called Boston butt or picnic pork)

1. Put the garlic, onions, parsley, 1 tablespoon salt, 1 tablespoon pepper, rum, sugar, and lime juice in a food processor fitted with the steel blade. Process until finely chopped, then drizzle in the oil, pulsing just to combine. Transfer the mixture to a small bowl.

2. Put the pork in a large bowl or on a platter big enough to hold it with the marinade. Vigorously rub the pork with the marinade, cover, and let marinate in the refrigerator for at least 4 hours or, preferably, overnight.

3. Preheat the oven to 400°F.

4. Put the pork on a rack in a large, heavy-bottomed roasting pan. Pour 1 cup water into the bottom of the pan to catch drippings. Put the pan in the oven and roast for 20 minutes. Lower the oven temperature to 350°F and continue roasting until an instant-read thermometer inserted to the

NIGHTLY SPECIALS

YOU CAN USE THIS RECIPE
to cook a 12-pound fresh ham;
double the marinade ingredients
and nearly triple the cooking time.

TO MAKE CUBAN SAND-
WICHES, fill soft rolls with thinly
sliced pork, ham, pickles, and
queso blanco and press with a
spatula in a hot pan or in a
sandwich press.

thickest part of the pork reads 155°F, 1½ to 2 hours. As it cooks, baste the
pork with any marinade remaining in the bowl.

5. Remove the pan from the oven, transfer the pork to a cutting board,
and let it rest for 20 minutes.

6. Carve the pork into ¼-inch-thick slices, removing the string as you do.
If desired, pour the pan drippings into a measuring cup, degrease using a
basting bulb, and spoon the sauce over the sliced pork.

BARBECUED SPARE RIBS AND MANGO BARBECUE JAM

SERVES 6 TO 8

Barbecued spare ribs are a personal favorite that I enjoy serving with nontraditional sauces, like the mango jam here that provides a pleasing, sweet contrast to the meat.

1 cup vinegar

1 cup light brown sugar

2 tablespoons fine sea salt

1 tablespoon cracked black pepper

8 pounds pork spare ribs, left as whole racks

1 cup Mango Barbecue Jam (recipe follows)

NIGHTLY SPECIALS

USE BABY BACK RIBS or lamb spare ribs.

THE POACHING LIQUID can be altered to suit your taste: add cayenne pepper and/or tomato paste in small increments, or add some Coffee Barbecue Sauce (page 218) or your favorite barbecue sauce.

1.　Pour 4 quarts water into a pot large enough to hold the spare ribs. Add the vinegar, sugar, salt, and pepper. Bring to a boil over high heat, then lower the heat and cook at a simmer for 15 minutes to concentrate the flavor of the vinegar and sugar. Add the ribs to the boiling liquid, raise the heat to high, and when the liquid returns to a boil, lower the heat so the liquid is simmering and poach the ribs for 15 minutes. Drain the ribs and set them aside to cool. The ribs can be made to this point, covered, and refrigerated for up to 24 hours. Let come to room temperature before proceeding.

2.　Preheat the oven to 425°F or prepare an outdoor grill for grilling. Put the poached ribs in a pan with a rack, or directly over an outdoor fire. Cook, turning occasionally, until nicely crisp and caramelized, about 40 minutes in the oven and 25 to 30 minutes on the grill. Brush on the jam and cook for 2 more minutes, just to flavor the pork and caramelize the jam.

3.　Arrange the ribs on a platter and serve.

MANGO BARBECUE JAM

2 pounds firm mango (2 or 3 mangos), cut into ½-inch dice

1 cup sugar

1 jalapeño chile, seeded and finely diced

1 red bell pepper, seeded and cut into ¼-inch dice

¼ cup freshly squeezed lime juice

1. Put all the ingredients into a pot. Place over medium heat and cook, stirring occasionally, for 30 minutes. Remove and let cool completely. Transfer to a food processor fitted with the steel blade and pulse a few times to a chunky texture. Keep refrigerated until ready to use or serve.

TURKISH BRAISED LAMB SHANKS WITH ROASTED PLUMS

SERVES 4

LAMB SHANKS ARE A REAL BOON TO COOKS because they take very little work, but never fail to impress. When braised, they come out of the pot as big, bold, intensely flavored hunks of meat, and the braising liquid can be strained and/or reduced to make a sauce. The lamb shanks are seared, and then just simmer in the braising-liquid.

2 tablespoons paprika

2 tablespoons ground cumin

2 teaspoons ground cardamom

2 teaspoons ground cinnamon

1 teaspoon allspice

½ teaspoon ground cloves

Fine sea salt and freshly ground black pepper

Four 1- to 1½-pound lamb shanks

¼ cup olive oil

2 large onions, cut into small dice (about 2 cups)

1 pound plums, preferably Damson or Italian prune, quartered, stones removed

½ cup sugar

1 cup dry white wine

2 cups hot homemade chicken stock (page 69) or low-sodium, store-bought chicken broth

1. Stir together the paprika, cumin, cardamom, cinnamon, allspice, cloves, 1 teaspoon salt, and 1 teaspoon pepper in a bowl. Rub the spice mix into the lamb shanks, creating a spice covering that coats the lamb completely. Set aside.

2. Heat the oil in a large Dutch oven over medium heat. Add the onions and sauté them, stirring occasionally, until they begin to brown, about 6 minutes. Add the plums and sugar, stir, and cook until the plums are browned and wilted, about 10 minutes. Use a slotted spoon to transfer the onions and plums to a bowl and set them aside.

3. Put the seasoned shanks in the Dutch oven and brown them well on all sides, about 8 minutes, turning to brown thoroughly. Pour in the wine

OMIT THE SPICES (except for
salt and pepper) and add chopped
fresh tomatoes and fresh herbs to
the broth. Or use red wine instead
of white and add some smashed
garlic cloves.

and cook until reduced by half, about 8 minutes. Pour in the hot broth,
taste, and adjust the seasoning if necessary.

4.   Adjust the heat so the liquid is just barely simmering. Cover the Dutch
oven and cook until the lamb is so tender it pulls away from the bone with
just the tug of a fork, 1½ to 2 hours; add the onions and plums during the
final 15 minutes of cooking. Periodically lift the lid to make sure the liquid is
just barely simmering. If it's bubbling too aggressively, lower the temperature so that it doesn't all boil away but instead reduces to a thickened sauce.

5.   Use tongs to remove the shanks from the pot and transfer each one to
a large dinner plate or shallow bowl. Spoon some sauce over each shank,
being sure to include some onions and plums, and serve.

BONELESS ROAST LEG OF LAMB WITH FETA, OLIVES, AND EGGPLANT

SERVES 6 TO 8

So OFTEN, when we eat the food of other cultures, we rely on the old standbys. But it's fun to experiment with the flavors of another country, using them in our own unique way. This recipe, a nightly special I made at home one Easter, gathers together some well-known ingredients in Greek cuisine like lamb, feta cheese, olives, and eggplant and cooks them in a new way.

8 to 10 small baby eggplants or Italian eggplants, halved lengthwise

Fine sea salt and freshly ground black pepper

½ cup olive oil

One 7- to 8-pound leg of lamb, boned and butterflied

2 cups fresh breadcrumbs

1 cup tightly packed chopped flatleaf parsley

3 large garlic cloves, minced

½ pound Greek feta cheese, crumbled

½ pound Kalamata or other Mediterranean-style ripe black olives, pitted and coarsely chopped

2 tablespoons rosemary leaves

Juice of 1 lemon

Special equipment: metal skewers and butcher's twine to pin and tie the leg of lamb

1. Preheat the oven to 375°F. Season the cut sides of the eggplant with salt and pepper and drizzle 2 tablespoons of the oil over them. Set aside.

2. Lay the butterflied leg of lamb flat on a work surface, fat side down. Pound the lamb with a meat pounder to flatten it to an even thickness of about 1½ inches.

3. Put the breadcrumbs, parsley, garlic, feta, olives, rosemary, ¼ cup of the oil, and the lemon juice in a food processor fitted with the steel blade and pulse together to make a stuffing for the lamb. Spread the stuffing

NIGHTLY SPECIALS

STUFF THE LAMB WITH ANY VARIETY OF FILLINGS such as raisins and nuts or apricots and brandied, pitted cherries. Or adapt this stuffing by adding more garlic and parsley; rosemary and thyme; or omitting the cheese.

evenly along the center of the inside of the leg of lamb. Roll the lamb into a cylinder, sealing the stuffing within. Pin the roll closed with skewers and tie at 1-inch intervals with butcher's twine so that it does not open during cooking.

4. Season the outside of the lamb with salt and pepper and drizzle with the remaining 2 tablespoons oil. Put the lamb, seam side down, in a roasting pan with a rack and roast for 45 minutes. Add the eggplant to the roasting pan, skin side down. Roast until an instant-read thermometer inserted in the thickest part of the leg reads 130°F, about 35 minutes more.

5. Remove the lamb and eggplant from the oven and allow the roast to cool for 20 minutes before slicing.

6. When ready to serve, remove the skewers and string and cut the rolled leg at a slight bias into thick slices. Divide the lamb and eggplant evenly among 6 to 8 dinner plates and serve.

YOU WANT

Potato and Vegetable Side Dishes

FRIES WITH THAT?

The produce section is my first stop whenever I visit the market, because it is where my menu often begins. What sides will I serve? Will the main dish feature vegetables, and if so, what can I serve with it? Vegetables should be an accompanying partner to the meal, a complement to the center of the plate, and never the mere window dressing that the name "garnish" implies. I don't use garnishes in any meal and neither should you. Selecting a vegetable that is a perfect counterpoint to the meat or fish with which it will share a plate is one of the great and creative happy moments in cooking.

This is especially true for the nation of more serious cooking enthusiasts we have become. We now revere farm-fresh vegetables, looking for heirloom tomatoes and heritage legumes. Many of us think nothing of driving miles out of our way to find just the right fresh herbs. All of which is a very good thing. Since the food revolution of the 1970s and 1980s, we have been much more aware of the benefits, both in healthfulness and flavor, of fresh fruits and vegetables. And those vegetables are becoming more available to us every day, as the age of specialty supermarkets with their quality selection of fresh food expands to all parts of the nation.

Whether making the dishes in this chapter, or simply sautéing some spinach or even serving a raw-tomato salad, look for the freshest produce you can find, demanding that your greengrocer maintain the produce section accordingly: rotating deliveries so that the freshest is always available to you, with the old and brown leftover going into his trash and not yours. And take advantage of the variety of produce: even though I wasn't able to even put a dent into the list of commonly available vegetables out there with the recipes and ideas that follow, this chapter offers many opportunities to create your own nightly specials with the ever widening selection we have to choose from.

HERB-ROASTED NEW POTATOES

SERVES 4 TO 6 AS A SIDE DISH

ROASTED POTATOES ARE THE EXCEPTION that proves the rule: something that remains special, no matter how many times you've seen it or how often you eat it. Most roasted potato recipes put the herbs in the oven along with the potatoes, drying out the herbs' essential oils. I prefer a blast of fresh herb flavor in the finished dish, so make a quick herb butter that's drizzled over the potatoes once roasted. The potatoes should be of a uniform size so they cook evenly; it's generally best to leave smaller ones whole and halve or quarter the larger ones.

2 pounds small potatoes (Red Bliss, small whites, Yukon gold, Yellow Finns, or fingerlings), skin intact, left whole or cut to a uniform size

⅓ cup olive oil

3 tablespoons unsalted butter

2 garlic cloves, minced (about 2 tablespoons)

2 tablespoons minced thyme

¼ cup minced flat-leaf parsley

Fine sea salt and freshly ground black pepper

1. Preheat the oven to 375°F.

2. Preheat the pan in the oven for 10 minutes. Drizzle the potatoes with the oil in a bowl and toss gently to coat.

3. Put the potatoes in the hot pan, spreading them out in a single layer, and roast until crisp and a knife pierces easily to their center, about 45 minutes, shaking the pan to roll the potatoes so they brown evenly.

4. Remove the pan from the oven and turn the potatoes out onto a paper towel–lined surface to drain. Transfer to a serving dish and cover to keep warm. Set aside.

5. Melt the butter in a sauté pan over medium heat until it bubbles and froths. Add the garlic and sauté until a light golden brown, about 2 min-

TRY DIFFERENT POTATOES, cut uniformly if large or left whole if small, and mix them together for an assorted potato roast. Add other herbs or spices to the butter or change the butter to olive oil. Or leave the garlic and herb butter out altogether and drizzle just-roasted potatoes with some special oil, like walnut or hazelnut oil or green Tuscan extra virgin olive oil.

utes. Add the thyme and parsley, stir together quickly, and remove the pan from the heat.

6. Pour the garlic-herb butter over the potatoes, season with salt and pepper, and serve family style from the center of the table or alongside fish or meat dishes.

POTATO GRATIN

SERVES 6 TO 8 AS A SIDE DISH

POTATO GRATIN COULDN'T BE EASIER: thin slices of potato and a seasoned cream fused together by gentle baking. When I have the necessary ingredients on hand, I find that this side dish practically begs to be made. A little potato gratin goes a long way because of the combined richness of potato and butterfat, so serve it in small portions and let people help themselves to seconds or enjoy leftovers the next day. A gratin has a real old-fashioned charm to it, so I like to serve it alongside very traditional dishes like Herb-Roasted Capon (page 183) or Standing Rib of Beef (page 202).

2 tablespoons unsalted butter

2 garlic cloves, minced (about 2 tablespoons)

1½ cups heavy cream

Fine sea salt and freshly ground black pepper

Scant pinch freshly grated nutmeg

4 large Idaho or russet potatoes (about 2 pounds), peeled and held in a bowl of cold water

1. Preheat the oven to 325°F. Butter a 2-quart, flameproof gratin dish or 9-inch circular casserole.

2. Stir the garlic, cream, 1 teaspoon salt, ½ teaspoon pepper, and the nutmeg together in a small bowl. Set aside.

3. Dry the potatoes thoroughly and cut them into ⅛-inch-thick rounds, using a mandoline or very sharp knife and steady hand. Arrange half of the slices in an even, overlapping, circular pattern in the gratin dish, working from the inside out, and adding layers as you go. Pour half the seasoned cream over the potatoes and shake the dish gently to allow the cream to flow toward the bottom of the dish. Finish layering in the rest of the potatoes, then pour the remaining cream over the top and shake again.

4. Set the gratin dish on a cookie sheet to catch any overflow and bake until the top has browned to a rich, golden hue and the cream is bubbling

A GRATIN CAN BE AS CASUAL AND RUSTIC OR AS FANCY AS YOU LIKE. For the former, serve it from the center of the table, inviting everyone to help themselves to a serving. For a more formal occasion, cool the gratin for 20 minutes, cut individual portions with a biscuit cutter, and plate it alongside fish or meat.

ADD MUSHROOMS, blue cheese, onions, leeks, or chopped herbs.

along the edges, about 1 hour and 15 minutes. To test for doneness, insert the tip of a knife into the potatoes; any resistance indicates the potatoes need additional cooking time.

5.   Remove the gratin from the oven and allow to cool for 10 minutes before slicing and serving.

MASHED POTATOES

For such a fundamentally simple dish, there are a remarkable number of recipes for mashed potatoes. Some use hot milk or cream and cold butter. Some call for sour cream. Some call for extracting excess water from the potatoes by boiling them, then roasting them to dry in the oven for several minutes. I think mashed potatoes should be as easy to cook as they are to eat. This recipe calls for simply boiling and draining the potatoes before mashing them and stirring in a seasoned cream and butter mixture. Less starchy, boiling potatoes such as Yellow Finn or Yukon gold make the best mashed spuds.

3 pounds Yukon gold or Yellow Finn potatoes, peeled and cut into 1½-inch chunks

1 cup heavy cream

6 tablespoons (¾ stick) unsalted butter

Fine sea salt and freshly ground black pepper

1. Pour 4 quarts cold water over the potatoes in a large, heavy-bottomed pot and set over high heat. Bring to a boil and continue to boil until a knife pierces easily to the center of a potato chunk, about 20 minutes.

2. Meanwhile, put the cream, butter, 1 teaspoon salt, and ½ teaspoon pepper into a heavy-bottomed saucepan. Heat over medium heat until the butter melts, but do not allow the mixture to boil. Remove the pan from the heat and keep the mixture covered and warm.

3. When the potatoes are fully cooked, drain in a colander and let sit in the colander to allow any lingering water to run off.

4. While the potatoes are still hot (cold potatoes turn rubbery and starchy), mash with a potato masher or rice them. I prefer a potato ricer, which results in a creamier texture. If using a ricer, fill it halfway, press the potato pulp into a bowl, refill it halfway, and press again. Repeat until you've used all the potato.

5. Use a wooden spoon to stir the hot cream mixture into the potatoes and continue stirring until well incorporated.

6. Serve promptly or keep the mashed potatoes warm for up to 1 hour in a double boiler or in bowl covered with plastic wrap and set over another bowl filled halfway with hot water.

YOUR NIGHTLY SPECIALS

ROASTED GARLIC MASHED POTATOES: Preheat the oven to 325°F. Cut the top ½ inch off a head of garlic to expose the cloves. Place the garlic, cut side up, on a sheet of foil. Drizzle 2 teaspoons olive oil over the exposed garlic, season with salt and pepper, and fold the foil over the top, crimping it and forming a sealed parcel. Set the garlic on the oven's center rack and roast until the individual cloves are soft (a knife tip will pierce them easily), approximately 40 minutes. Remove the parcel from the oven and set aside to cool. When cool enough to handle, squeeze the cloves out of their skins and mash them to a paste with a fork. Stir the puree into the potatoes.

CHILE MASHED POTATOES: 1 to 2 tablespoons ancho chile paste or other dried chile powder rehydrated in boiling water to form a paste.

HORSERADISH AND GREEN ONION MASHED POTATOES: Stir ¼ cup fresh grated horseradish root and ½ cup chopped scallions into the mashed potatoes.

THE BEST FRIES YOU'VE EVER MADE!

SERVES 4 AS A SIDE DISH OR HORS D'OEUVRES

FRENCH FRIES ARE A REAL TREAT. Who doesn't love them? Great French fries are rare even in restaurants, so imagine how much pleasure can be had by cook and diner alike when they're made at home. The key is double-frying the potatoes, once to ensure the inside is cooked and remains fluffy; a second time to achieve maximum crunch. I often serve French fries as an hors d'oeuvres with dipping sauces like curried or chile mayonnaise, or make them the focus of a fondue by accompanying them with a pot of melted cheddar cheese sauce.

Stovetop fryers can be dangerous because of the open flame, so I recommend that you make these with an electric deep-fryer with an adjustable thermostat. Buy the biggest one you can afford so you can cook a large quantity of fries (or egg rolls, or whatever) rapidly.

Peanut or vegetable oil, for frying (if you dare, add 50 percent beef lard or suet to the oil for more robust flavor)

3 pounds Idaho or russet potatoes, peeled

Fine sea salt

1. Preheat the oil in the fryer to 245°F.

2. Either by hand or using a French-fry cutter, cut even fries ¼ inch square and 5 or 6 inches long, gathering them in a bowl of cold water as you work.

3. When the oil is hot and ready to cook, drain the fries of all water and pat thoroughly dry with paper towels. (This is critical. Water and salt are the enemies of frying oil. The fries can sit on paper towels for a few minutes, in a single layer, to air-dry if you're not sure you've gotten all the water out.) Once they're dry, add just enough fries to the fryer basket to fill it halfway. This will ensure even cooking without allowing the frying oil temperature to drop too much, which results in greasy fries.

This first fry is also called blanching, since it's not meant to add any color. The fries will only be par-cooked and their color will change only

FOR SEASONED FRIES, sprinkle a combination of sea salt with chili powder for chili fries or paprika for mildly seasoned fries.

from raw white to slightly creamier color. The batch of fries is done when they appear to be a more yellow-white than raw-white color, about 5 minutes. Remove each batch, drain of all oil, and spread out on paper towels to cool.

4. After all fries have been blanched, they will hold for several hours. Refrigerate them, covered, if you like, but do not freeze them.

5. Bring the fryer to 365°F to 385°F. (It can be the same oil, but only reuse it once.) Cook the blanched fries a second time in batches in this hot oil. Do not overload the fryer; each batch should fill the basket halfway. Fry each batch to a rich, golden-brown color. Time will vary from 2 to 3 minutes, depending on the fryer and the speed with which it reheats. For crispier fries, fry a bit longer. Drain and salt each batch as soon as it's done and keep it covered and warm while you fry the remaining batches.

6. Serve the fries piping hot alongside the dish of your choice or on their own.

Note: If you don't have an electric deep fryer, heat the oil in a 5-quart cast-iron stovetop fryer and use a large strainer to ladle the fries out of the fryer.

SWEET POTATO HASH

SERVES 4 TO 6 AS A SIDE DISH

THIS IS A HASH, NOT A MASH: the cubed sweet potatoes should be cooked through but still maintain their shape. The parboiling should just warm them and the sautéing should finish the job and crisp the exterior.

Fine sea salt and freshly ground black pepper

About 2 pounds sweet potatoes or yams, peeled and cut into ½-inch dice (about 3 cups)

¼ cup canola oil

4 tablespoons (½ stick) unsalted butter

2 large onions, cut into ½-inch dice

¼ cup maple syrup

1 teaspoon ground cinnamon

1. Bring a large, heavy-bottomed pot of salted water to a boil over high heat. Add the diced potatoes and parboil them for 3 minutes. Drain them in a colander, refresh under cold running water, drain again, and set aside to cool at room temperature.

2. Meanwhile, heat the oil and 1 tablespoon of the butter in a sauté pan over medium heat. Add the onions and sauté until richly browned and caramel-colored, 7 to 8 minutes. Remove the pan from the heat and set aside to cool at room temperature. Once the potatoes and onions are cool, put them both in a mixing bowl. (The dish can be prepared to this stage, covered, and refrigerated overnight. Let come to room temperature before proceeding.)

3. Add the syrup and cinnamon and season with pepper. Gently stir the hash to ensure uniform seasoning and set aside.

USE BROWN SUGAR instead of maple syrup or add pumpkin spices (mace, allspice, cloves, and nutmeg) in addition to the cinnamon.

PUT THE COOKED HASH INTO A PIECRUST SHELL, pour 1 cup cream whisked with 4 eggs over the top, and bake at 350°F until set, about 40 minutes, to make a sweet potato pie similar to a quiche.

4. Melt the remaining 3 tablespoons butter in a nonstick sauté pan over medium heat. Add the potato-onion mixture and cook until browned and the potatoes and onions begin to adhere to one another, about 9 minutes.

5. Transfer the hash to a serving dish and present family style from the center of the table.

GARLIC-ROASTED YUCA

SERVES 4 TO 6 AS A SIDE DISH

Yuca, a starchy root vegetable, is popular on tables from Brazil to the Caribbean. Also known as manioc, this starchy, slightly sweet vegetable boils, mashes, and fries beautifully, and is a nice change from potatoes. This is especially delicious with roasted poultry and meats such as Charred Beef Medallions (page 206) and Grilled Pork Chops with Coffee Barbecue Sauce (page 217).

2 pounds yuca

Fine sea salt and freshly ground black pepper

1 tablespoon ground cumin

½ pound bacon, coarsely chopped

3 tablespoons olive oil

4 garlic cloves, minced

½ cup dried breadcrumbs

¼ cup chopped almonds

1. Preheat the oven to 375°F.

2. Cut the yuca into 3-inch pieces. Peel off the brown skin with a sharp paring knife. Cut the yuca pieces in half and set aside in a bowl of cold water.

3. Fill a heavy-bottomed pot with enough water to cover the yuca. Bring the water to a boil over high heat. Add 1½ teaspoons salt to the water, add the yuca to the pot, and return the water to a boil. Lower the heat and let the yuca simmer until softened, about 15 minutes. Drain the yuca and let rest until cool enough to handle. Use a sharp knife to remove any thick fibers from the center core of the yuca.

4. Put the yuca in a vegetable roasting dish and sprinkle evenly with the cumin and 1 teaspoon black pepper.

5. Meanwhile, sauté the bacon in a heavy-bottomed sauté pan over medium heat until the fat has been rendered and the bacon is crisp, about

AFTER BOILING THE YUCA you can proceed to any other cooking technique you like, such as cutting and frying them according to the directions on page 238. Or, mash the yuca as you would mashed potatoes with cream and butter. The mashed yuca can be formed into small patties and shallow-fried to a crisp finish on both sides.

8 minutes. Use a slotted spoon to transfer the bacon to a paper towel–lined plate to drain, leaving the fat in the pan.

6. Add the oil to the bacon fat and warm slowly. Add the garlic and toast it to a pale golden brown, about 2 minutes. Pour the garlic and oil over the yuca in the roasting dish. Add the cooked bacon to the yuca and stir to combine evenly.

7. Combine the breadcrumbs with the chopped nuts and sprinkle on top of the yuca. Put the dish in the oven and roast until the top is browned and crisp, about 25 minutes.

8. Serve the yuca family style from the center of the table.

COUNTRY BREAD STUFFING WITH ONIONS AND SAGE

SERVES 6 TO 8 AS A SIDE DISH

I LOVE TURKEY AND I LOVE STUFFING, but I never cook them together; they cook at different rates and if cooked in the cavity of the bird, the stuffing prevents the turkey from receiving the proper amount of heat for a good roasting. The turkey breast usually gets overcooked because the heat cannot reach the breast through the cavity fast enough. Since I don't cook stuffing in the turkey, I see no need to wait for Thanksgiving to make it. Put day-old bread to use in something that everybody loves and that will be more special on days other than the last Thursday in November.

About 4 tablespoons (½ stick) unsalted butter

1 medium onion, cut into small dice (about 1 cup)

½ cup raw, crumbled country sausage

3 tablespoons chopped sage

6 cups day-old country bread cut into 1-inch cubes

1½ cups homemade chicken stock (page 69) or low-sodium, store-bought chicken broth

½ cup milk

3 eggs

Fine sea salt and freshly ground black pepper

1.   Preheat the oven to 350°F.

2.   Melt 2 tablespoons of the butter in a sauté pan set over medium-high heat. Add the onion and sauté until softened but not browned, about 4 minutes. Add the sausage, stir, and cook until browned, about 5 minutes. Stir in the sage and remove the pan from the heat. Set aside and let cool completely.

3.   Stir together the bread, cooled onion mixture, stock, milk, and eggs in a bowl to combine well. Season with salt and pepper. Spoon the mixture

ADD 1 CUP DICED APPLES to the onion and sausage and cook together before mixing with the bread. Leave out the sausage and add 1 cup shucked oysters to make an oyster-flavored stuffing.

into a baking dish. Dot the top of the stuffing with the remaining 2 tablespoons butter, adding more butter if you like.

4.   Bake until the top is crusty and well browned and the stuffing is crisped around the edges, 35 to 40 minutes.

5.   Serve either in the casserole dish or spooned into a serving dish.

SAVORY CHIPOTLE CHILE MUFFINS

SERVES 6 TO 8 AS A SIDE DISH

Wʜᴀᴛ ɪɴ ᴛʜᴇ ᴡᴏʀʟᴅ ɪs ᴀ sᴀᴠᴏʀʏ ᴍᴜꜰꜰɪɴ? An "unsweet-ened" one that's meant to be served with lunch or dinner rather than with breakfast or as a dessert. The English Yorkshire pudding, made by baking a flour batter in a muffin tin coated with hot beef drippings, paved the way for this type of muffin. These Southwestern muffins, flavored with smoky chipotle chiles, will be a welcome surprise alongside dishes such as Texas-Style Oven-Barbecued Beef Brisket (page 200) or Charred Beef Medallions with Poblano-Tequila Sauce (page 206).

6 eggs

1½ cups milk

5 tablespoons unsalted butter, melted but not browned

2 cups all-purpose flour

½ cup cornmeal

1 tablespoon plus 1½ teaspoons baking powder

Fine sea salt and freshly ground black pepper

2 tablespoons chipotle in adobo sauce, blended to a paste (puree 1 whole chile, adding just enough can juices to make a paste)

1 tablespoon ground cumin

NIGHTLY SPECIALS

USE SOME BEEF DRIPPINGS from the Standing Rib of Beef (page 202) in place of the melted butter.

ADD OTHER SAVORY INGREDI-ENTS, such as 1 tablespoon sesame seeds or 3 tablespoons chopped pecans, to the batter.

1. Preheat the oven 425°F.

2. Beat the eggs, milk, and butter together in a bowl until smooth.

3. Stir together the flour, cornmeal, baking powder, 1 teaspoon salt, 1 teaspoon pepper, the chipotle paste, and cumin in another bowl to combine well. Pour the egg-milk-butter mixture into this mixture, stirring to incorporate and avoid lumps.

4. Pour the batter into the wells of a nonstick 15-muffin tin, filling each well three-quarters of the way up its side.

5. Bake the muffins until they rise and are golden brown, about 35 minutes.

6. Transfer the muffins to a linen napkin–lined basket and serve warm from the oven.

CARDAMOM AND FENNEL-SCENTED CARROTS

SERVES 4 TO 6 AS A SIDE DISH

So MANY OF US GREW UP on crinkle-cut carrots from a can or frozen bag that we forget how special carrots can be with just a little cooking to coax out their sweetness and some well-chosen accompaniments. Here, carrots are glazed with honey and imbued with the aroma and flavor of cardamom and fennel seeds. They reach the table tasting almost like candy. Try to only use "fresh" carrots, that is, those that are still sprouting their green tops. This is an indication that they are truly fresh and not of the storage variety, which can be excessively starchy and missing that true carrot flavor.

1 pound carrots, peeled and sliced diagonally crosswise into ¼-inch-thick slices

2 tablespoons unsalted butter

3 tablespoons honey

1½ teaspoons ground cardamom

1½ teaspoons fennel seeds

½ teaspoon fine sea salt

½ teaspoon freshly ground black pepper

Fresh cilantro, optional, for garnish

1. Put all of the ingredients except the cilantro plus ⅓ cup water into a sauté pan and stir to coat the carrots evenly. Bring to a boil and steam, covered, until the carrots are just tender, but not overcooked, about 5 minutes.

2. Remove the cover of the sauté pan and continue to cook over medium-high heat, stirring to keep the seeds and spices from scorching, until the carrots are nicely glazed and tender but still a bit al dente, about 2 minutes more.

3. Transfer the carrots to a serving dish, garnish with cilantro, if using, and serve family style from the center of the table.

FOR A TRULY EXOTIC SIDE DISH, use peeled salsify instead of carrots. Make the dish using equal parts parsnips and carrots for a colorful alternative.

USE CURRY OR GROUND CUMIN as the spice.

ADD SUGAR, MAPLE SYRUP, OR EVEN CANE SUGAR to the pan to glaze the carrots. Try adding fresh dill and celery salt at the end; they will transform the flavor dramatically.

GLAZED WHOLE-ROASTED SHALLOTS

IF YOU THINK OF SHALLOTS only as something to be sliced or minced and tossed in with other ingredients, then whole-roasted shallots will be a revelation. I start the shallots in the pan to caramelize them before roasting them to a soft, succulent state. I serve them as a side dish to game and roasted beef.

16 to 24 large shallots or very small onions (about 1 pound)

3 tablespoons unsalted butter

3 tablespoons sugar

Fine sea salt and freshly ground black pepper

½ cup homemade chicken stock (page 69) or low sodium, store-bought chicken broth

1 tablespoon thyme leaves

YOUR NIGHTLY SPECIALS

TRY THIS WITH PEARL ONIONS, but reduce the cooking time by a few minutes. Cippolini onions are small, flat onions (actually the bulbs of a hyacinth plant) that have a floral aroma. If you can find them, cook them in the same way.

ADD ¼ CUP RED WINE to the broth.

1. Preheat the oven to 350°F.

2. Peel the papery skin off the shallots, being careful not to cut or tear but to leave them as whole as possible.

3. Melt the butter in a wide, heavy-bottomed sauté pan over medium heat until it begins to bubble. Add the shallots, shaking the pan to coat them with butter. Brown them all over until nicely caramelized to a rich, golden-brown color, 6 to 8 minutes. Sprinkle with the sugar, ½ teaspoon salt, and a few grinds of pepper. Pour in the stock, raise the heat to high, and bring to a boil.

4. Pour the contents of the pan into a small casserole or baking dish and roast for 5 minutes. Stir the shallots and, if the liquid has evaporated, add a few tablespoons water. Continue cooking until the liquid has evaporated and the shallots have caramelized to a rich dark golden brown and are tender when pierced with a knife, about 10 more minutes.

5. Transfer the shallots to a serving dish, stir in the thyme, and serve family style from the center of the table.

CREAMED SPINACH WITH BACON

SERVES 4 AS A SIDE DISH

CREAMED SPINACH is a usual side dish offered at steak houses. Making your own creamed spinach is not time consuming and the results are superior to even the best you've ever had. The secret? Fresh spinach. This version was one of the specials served more than seventy-five years ago at '21' on opening night.

6 slices bacon

4 to 6 cups fresh spinach leaves, well washed in several changes of cold water

2 tablespoons unsalted butter

2 tablespoons all-purpose flour

½ cup heavy cream

Fine sea salt and freshly ground black pepper

2 pinches freshly grated nutmeg

1. Heat a nonstick sauté pan over low heat. Put in the bacon and sauté until crispy, about 8 minutes. Use tongs to transfer the bacon to a paper towel–lined plate to drain. Once it's cool enough to handle, crumble the bacon into small bits and set aside. Reserve the bacon fat.

2. Bring 2 inches water to a simmer in a vegetable steamer over medium heat. Put the spinach in the steamer basket, cover, and steam until cooked, about 2 minutes.

3. Transfer the spinach to a colander to drain and let the spinach cool slightly. Squeeze out any excess water. Transfer the spinach onto a cutting board and roughly chop with a sharp knife.

4. Heat the butter and 2 tablespoons reserved bacon fat in a heavy-bottomed saucepan over medium-high heat until it melts and begins to bubble. Whisk the flour into the butter and cook together for 2 to 3 minutes.

5. In a separate pot, heat the cream until steaming but not boiling.

NIGHTLY SPECIALS

PUT CREAMED SPINACH IN
A CASSEROLE DISH, top with
breadcrumbs, and bake until bubbly and the crust on top is golden,
about 15 minutes.

6. Whisk the cream into the flour-butter mixture and bring it to a boil over high heat. Immediately lower the heat and let simmer until thickened, 2 to 3 minutes.

7. Add the spinach to the cream and cook for 5 minutes. Season to taste with salt, pepper, and nutmeg and stir in the bacon.

8. Transfer the creamed spinach to a serving bowl and serve hot.

BITTER GREENS AND HONEY ALMONDS

SERVES 4 AS A SIDE DISH

THIS RECIPE CAN BE MADE with any or all of the following: mustard greens, collard greens, kale, escarole, or beet greens. It's not just that eating these things are good for you, but that their rich, earthy flavors serve as counterpoint to fatty meats and protein, help the palate recover, and ready us for the next bite.

6 slices bacon, diced

2 pounds mustard or other greens, well washed in several changes of cold water and

chopped or shredded by hand into small pieces

3 tablespoons unsalted butter

1 cup whole almonds

½ cup honey

Fine sea salt and freshly ground black pepper

YOUR NIGHTLY SPECIALS

USE SMOKED HAM instead of bacon.

ADD SMOKED FISH, like mackerel, to the greens to make this a side dish to shrimp. Or add smoked turkey breast instead.

USE KALE and Swiss chard together.

FINISH THE DISH by tossing in a pinch of crushed red pepper flakes.

1. Cook the diced bacon in a sauté pan over medium-low heat until the fat has rendered and the bacon is crispy, 6 to 8 minutes. Drain the bacon on a paper towel–lined plate and set aside.

2. Cover the greens with cold water in a pot and cook until tender, 20 minutes for mustard greens, 90 minutes for collard greens, 10 minutes for broccoli rabe, 10 minutes for escarole, and 15 minutes for beet greens. Drain the greens and set aside.

3. In a wide, heavy-bottomed sauté pan, heat the butter and add the almonds. Sauté until they start to brown, 3 minutes. Pour in ½ cup water, then the honey. Stir and cook until the water has evaporated and the honey has caramelized and coated the almonds, about 5 minutes. Before the almonds become too dry, add the cooked greens and bacon, season with salt and pepper and cook, tossing and stirring, to evenly distribute the almonds and bacon.

4. Serve at once.

BRAISED KALE WITH RED WINE

SERVES 6 TO 8 AS A SIDE DISH

THIS IS SUCH A FULL-FLAVORED *and textured dish that it almost dictates the rest of the meal: serve it with assertively flavored roasted and grilled fish and meat.*

3 tablespoons olive oil

1 large clove garlic, thinly sliced

1 large bunch kale (about 2 pounds), wilted leaves, stems, and tough center stalks removed,

well washed, drained, and cut into 2-inch pieces

½ cup full-bodied red wine such as Shiraz

Fine sea salt and freshly ground black pepper

¼ teaspoon crushed red pepper flakes

Meat from 1 cooked ham hock (about 1 cup)

NIGHTLY SPECIALS

REMOVE ½ POUND SWEET, FRESH ITALIAN OR PORTUGUESE SAUSAGE FROM ITS CASING. Heat a sauté pan over medium heat, add the sausage, and brown until done and slightly crisped. Add the sausage to the kale during the final 2 minutes of cooking.

1. Heat the oil in a large, heavy-bottomed sauté pan over low heat. Add the garlic and sauté for 1 minute. Add the kale and sauté for 2 to 3 minutes. Add the wine, 1 teaspoon salt, 1 teaspoon pepper, the pepper flakes, and ham. Stir and cover the pan to braise with the wine. Cook until the kale is tender, about 10 minutes.

2. Transfer the kale to a serving dish and serve family style from the center of the table.

ROASTED ASPARAGUS WITH PARMIGIANO-REGGIANO

SERVES 6 TO 8 AS A SIDE DISH

ASPARAGUS AND PARMIGIANO-REGGIANO have a natural affinity for each other; the saltiness of the cheese mingles perfectly with the fresh, green flavor of the vegetable. While steamed asparagus on its own is certainly a popular side dish, roasted asparagus with melted cheese is a bit more special and requires almost no additional work. I prefer to avoid winter asparagus, which I find lacking in real spring flavor. I wait for fresh asparagus in the spring.

2 tablespoons plus ½ teaspoon freshly squeezed lemon juice

Fine sea salt and freshly ground black pepper

2 pounds jumbo asparagus, ends trimmed, stalks peeled to within 2 inches of the tip

2 tablespoons olive oil

4 ounces Parmigiano-Reggiano, grated (1 cup)

NIGHTLY SPECIALS

TRY GRILLING THE COOLED, BLANCHED ASPARAGUS, drizzled with oil, on an outdoor barbecue for 2 minutes, until nicely charred with smoky flavor. Sprinkle with cheese as you serve. Or put the oil-drizzled asparagus under a preheated oven broiler and char somewhat before sprinkling on the cheese to melt under the broiler.

1. Preheat the oven to 450°F. Fill a large bowl halfway with ice water.

2. Pour the 2 tablespoons lemon juice into a heavy-bottomed pot with 4 cups water, season with salt and pepper, and bring to a boil over high heat. Tie the asparagus into small bundles with kitchen twine for easier handling.

3. Poach the asparagus in the boiling liquid until crisp-tender, about 2 minutes, being careful not to overcook them. Drain the asparagus and submerge in the ice water to stop the blanching process. Untie the asparagus bundles. The asparagus can be drained and refrigerated at this point for up to 1 day.

4. Put the asparagus in a large, flat baking dish. Drizzle with olive oil and the remaining ½ teaspoon lemon juice. Sprinkle the Parmigiano-Reggiano over the asparagus and roast until the cheese melts, about 6 minutes.

5. Serve immediately.

ROASTED CHESTNUTS AND BRUSSELS SPROUTS

Dozens of desserts *feature sweetened chestnut puree, but consider chestnuts on the dinner table as a seductive accompaniment to capon and turkey.*

Fine sea salt and freshly ground black pepper

1 pound Brussels sprouts, outer leaves removed, bottoms trimmed

4 tablespoons (½ stick) unsalted butter

3 tablespoons minced shallots

1 pound peeled roasted chestnuts, halved and thinly sliced

1 cup homemade chicken stock (page 69) or low-sodium, store-bought chicken broth

2 tablespoons chopped rosemary

2 tablespoons chopped thyme

1. Bring 2 quarts water to a boil in a large, heavy-bottomed pot over high heat. Salt the water, add the Brussels sprouts, and cook until tender, 10 to 12 minutes. Drain, refresh in cold water, and pat dry with paper towels. Cut in half.

2. Heat the butter in a large, heavy-bottomed sauté pan over medium heat for 1 minute. Add the shallots and sauté for 1 minute. Add the chestnuts and Brussels sprouts and sauté for 3 to 4 minutes. Add the broth, bring to a boil over high heat, lower the heat, and cook at a simmer for 5 minutes. Add the rosemary and thyme and season with salt and pepper.

3. Transfer the chestnuts and Brussels sprouts to a serving bowl and serve hot.

Fresh chestnuts

Fresh chestnuts are available in very limited supply in late fall to early winter. You can buy peeled, blanched, and Cryovac-packed chestnuts in many markets. Use them if you can, or peel your own; they're very simple to prepare. I always have fresh chestnuts in my home from Thanksgiving through the New Year. I cut an X in the flat side of the shell with a sharp knife, roast them in a 375°F oven for 6 to 8 minutes, and cool them for 5 minutes, before peeling and eating them out of hand.

FRESH GREEN PEAS WITH BOSTON LETTUCE

SERVES 6 AS A SIDE DISH

SERVED SLIGHTLY WARMED AND WILTED, as it is here, lettuce's mild and buttery flavor comes through, making it a fine partner for fresh peas.

Fine sea salt and freshly ground black pepper

2 cups shelled fresh green peas, rinsed in cold water and drained

4 tablespoons (½ stick) unsalted butter

6 to 8 leaves Boston, Bibb, or Limestone lettuce, sliced into julienne

YOUR NIGHTLY SPECIALS

ADD ½ CUP DICED COOKED HAM and/or fresh herbs like tarragon to perk up the flavor even more.

1. Bring 2 cups water to a boil in a heavy-bottomed pot over high heat. Salt the water, add the peas, and cook until tender, 3 to 4 minutes.

2. Drain the peas and return them to the warm pot. Add the butter and stir the peas gently to help melt it. Stir in the lettuce, cook 2 minutes more, season with salt and pepper, and serve.

GINGERED GREEN BEANS

SERVES 4 AS A SIDE DISH

As DELICIOUS AS GREEN BEANS *can be steamed or sautéed on their own or in salads, I find them more interesting when cooked with bold ingredients. They take on the character of other ingredients without sacrificing their own crunch and clean fresh flavor.*

Fine sea salt and freshly ground black pepper

1 pound fresh green beans, trimmed to uniform length

3 tablespoons vegetable oil

2 tablespoons chopped pickled ginger

1 tablespoon chopped garlic

2 or 3 whole, small, dried hot chiles, such as bird's eye

YOUR NIGHTLY SPECIALS

USE FRESH GINGER for a more sprightly flavor.

ADD SOME CHINESE FER-MENTED BLACK BEANS for a salty, pungent, and authentic Asian taste.

ADD SOME SESAME OIL to the finished dish.

ADD SOME SLICED ROASTED CHICKEN to turn this into a warm salad.

1.   Bring 2 cups water to a boil in a heavy-bottomed pot over high heat, salt the water, and add the beans. Boil until crisp-tender, about 6 minutes. Drain the beans and let cool slightly.

2.   Heat the oil in a large, heavy-bottomed sauté pan over medium-high heat. Add the ginger, garlic, and chiles and sauté for 1 minute. Add the beans and sauté for 2 minutes, stirring. Use tongs to remove the chiles. Adjust the seasoning with salt and pepper and serve.

JUST

Simple Sweets and Grand Finales

DESSERTS

Desserts are creative and whimsical, and fittingly so because their goal is one thing and one thing only—pleasure, pure and simple. You don't need dessert in the same way that you do a steak or dish of black beans, as delicious and sensual as they may be. I believe that dessert recipes intended for the home kitchen should be relatively easy to prepare. Pastry making is a realm unto itself; many passionate amateur pastry chefs out there can make puff pastry from scratch, and in their hands a pastry bag is an instrument of art, but my recipes shy away from intricateness in favor of accessibility. They are of the comforting and comfortable home variety: pies, cobblers, a mousse or two, and so on. Sure, some are more challenging than others, but they are all eminently makeable. And they all fulfill the one requirement of any dessert: pure, sweet, delicious satisfaction.

DOUBLE-CRUST APPLE PIE

MAKES 1 PIE, ENOUGH TO SERVE 6 TO 8

THE QUINTESSENTIAL AMERICAN DESSERT, *apple pie is ubiquitous, available everywhere from roadside diners to fast-food chains to country fairs and neighborhood restaurants. But it shouldn't be overlooked or taken for granted, because there's a lot to be said for a treat that's so universally adored. What's more, with so many varieties of heirloom and heritage apples available every year, I never tire of making the Great American Dessert from scratch for family and friends, tweaking the recipe a little every time.*

6 tablespoons (¾ stick) unsalted butter

2½ pounds firm, tart apples (preferably seasonal local specials like Macouns, Northern Spy, or Granny Smith), peeled, cored, and sliced into ¼-inch wedges

½ cup sugar plus 1 tablespoon for sprinkling

¼ cup raisins

½ teaspoon ground cinnamon

¼ teaspoon ground cloves

2 tablespoons freshly squeezed lemon juice

2 tablespoons cornstarch

Basic Pie Dough (page 266)

1 egg, beaten with 2 tablespoons water to make an egg wash

1. Melt 3 tablespoons of the butter in a large, heavy-bottomed sauté pan over medium heat. Add the apple wedges and sauté until slightly softened but holding their shape, 3 to 4 minutes. Add the sugar and stir to combine. Add the raisins, cinnamon, and cloves and stir.

2. In a bowl, combine the lemon juice and cornstarch. Stir the mixture into the apple mixture and remove the pan from the heat. Let cool completely.

3. Preheat the oven to 375°F.

4. Fill an unbaked bottom crust with apple filling and dot the top with the remaining 3 tablespoons butter. Top with a rolled-out top crust. Cut ½-inch vents in a round-the-clock pattern into the top crust to allow steam to escape. Brush the top lightly with egg wash and sprinkle with the remaining 1 tablespoon sugar.

VARY THE VARIETY OF APPLE or use pears or peaches.

VARY THE SPICES and/or serve this with homemade ice cream or aged cheddar cheese melted on top.

5. Put the pie on a cookie sheet or other low-sided baking tray to catch any spillage. Place on the middle rack of the oven and bake for 20 minutes, checking occasionally to ensure that the top is browning evenly. Rotate the pie 180 degrees to move the front edge to the back of the oven, and bake until the top is uniformly golden brown, 15 to 20 more minutes.

6. Remove the pie from the oven and let cool for 20 minutes before slicing and serving.

BASIC PIE DOUGH

MAKES TWO 10-INCH PIECRUSTS, ENOUGH FOR 1 DOUBLE-CRUST PIE OR
2 SINGLE-CRUST PIES

EVERY COOK SHOULD HAVE one or two desserts he can whip up on the spur of the moment and pies are one of those not too difficult to master, did-you-really-make-this? recipes that can be adapted in almost endless ways. This dough may be used as a bottom crust only, giving you an extra one to freeze until needed. It can also be used as a "blind baked" pie shell bottom—a par-baked, empty bottom crust to be filled later. Just remember to use pie weights when blind baking.

Make the time to relax and enjoy the sensual aspect of dough making. The cardinal rule is to not allow dough to get warm, either in the bowl by the heat of your hands, or by letting it sit out at room temperature. To prevent this, use ice-cold butter and refrigerate the dough until ready to bake.

2½ cups all-purpose flour, plus more for dusting a work surface

¼ teaspoon baking powder

Fine sea salt

½ pound (2 sticks) cold unsalted butter, cut into cubes, plus more for greasing the dish

About ⅓ cup ice-cold water

1 egg yolk, beaten with 2 tablespoons water to make an egg wash (if making a top crust)

1. Put the flour and baking powder in a food processor and pulse to combine. Add the cold butter cubes and pulse a few times until the mixture begins to become mealy and the butter forms plainly visible pea-size nuggets.

2. Dissolve ½ teaspoon salt in the water. With the motor running, pour in the water and let mix, just until the dough pulls together. Do not overmix the dough; if it appears dry and is not holding together, add a few additional tablespoons of water.

3. Form the dough into a ball, flatten it, wrap it in plastic wrap, and refrigerate until ready to use. (If making another recipe that calls for this dough, refer to that recipe at this point. Otherwise, follow the remaining instructions.)

4. Lightly flour a pastry board and a rolling pin and unwrap the dough. Divide the dough into 2 equal pieces and keep the second piece refrigerated. Tamp down the dough with the rolling pin and gently begin to roll it out into a circular pie shape by rolling evenly outward from the center, working quickly, and turning the dough in one-eighth turns to keep the rolling even. When the dough is rolled out to an even thickness of about ⅛ inch and is about 12 inches in diameter, it is ready to be transferred to a 10-inch pie dish. (I prefer to use Pyrex glass pie dishes; they transmit heat uniformly, don't warp like tins, and let you see how the bottom crust is progressing during baking.)

5. Lightly butter the dish, lift the dough with the rolling pin by partially rolling the dough up on the pin, center the dough in the dish, and unroll. Pierce the dough in several places with the tines of a fork.

6. Roll the second half of the pie dough into a circle slightly larger than the pie dish. Fill the bottom crust with your chosen filling. Cover the filling with the top half of the dough. Using both hands, crimp the edges of the two crusts together to seal. With a sharp knife, make several crosshatch slits in the top crust. Brush with the egg wash and bake in a preheated 375°F oven for 35 to 40 minutes. Remove from the oven and cool for 20 minutes.

TRIPLE BERRY AND PECAN CRUNCH PIE

MAKES A 10-INCH PIE, ENOUGH TO SERVE 6 TO 8

As SATISFYING AS BLUEBERRIES AND BLACKBERRIES are on their own, they take on a new dimension when baked in a pie. My first taste of triple-berry pie was at a San Francisco restaurant where I became an instant, lifetime fan of bottom-crust-only pie. In this version, the crunch topping resembles a crumb cake with nuts, an irresistible companion to the berries.

1½ cups all-purpose flour, plus more for dusting a work surface

½ recipe Basic Pie Dough (page 266; bottom crust only)

3 pints blueberries, blackberries, strawberries, or a combination

1½ cups sugar

2 tablespoons cornstarch

½ teaspoon peeled, grated fresh ginger, or ¼ teaspoon ground ginger

2 tablespoons ground cinnamon

¼ teaspoon ground nutmeg

Juice and grated zest of 1 orange

Juice and grated zest of 1 lemon

½ cup day-old pound cake crumbs, or ½ cup white bread crumbs

½ cup chopped pecans, optional

12 tablespoons (1½ sticks) cold unsalted butter, cut into pieces

1. Preheat the oven to 375°F.

2. Flour a work surface and roll the pie dough out to the size and shape of a 10-inch pie dish. Lay the dough in the dish and prick the bottom with the tines of a fork. Refrigerate for 30 minutes. Cover the pie dough with a piece of parchment paper and weight it down with pie-dough weights or clean, dry beans. Bake for 8 minutes. Remove from the oven, remove the beans and paper, and set aside to cool thoroughly.

3. Put the berries, 1 cup of the sugar, the cornstarch, ginger, 1 tablespoon of the cinnamon, the nutmeg, orange juice and zest, and lemon juice and zest in a bowl and mix well. Sprinkle the cake crumbs on the bottom of the

THIS IS A VERSATILE RECIPE: change to any fruit you prefer. If you use stone fruit like peaches, plums, or nectarines, heat the filling in a saucepan for 5 minutes before transferring it to the pie shell. If using other berries, the greater the selection, the more interesting this pie will be. In the height of summer, add huckleberries and whatever wild berries you can get your hands on.

pre-baked piecrust. Fill the pie shell with the berry mixture and bake in the oven until the filling begins to bubble slightly, 15 to 20 minutes.

4. While the pie is baking, stir together in a bowl the pecans, if using, the flour, the remaining ½ cup sugar, and the remaining tablespoon cinnamon. Stir the butter gently in the bowl and rub 1 cube at a time in your hands to form peanut-size nuggets for the crunch.

5. Sprinkle the crunch over the top of the pie, reduce the oven temperature to 350°F, and bake until the filling bubbles out of the crust, about 30 more minutes. If the crunch begins to darken too quickly, cover with aluminum foil. Let the pie cool at room temperature for at least 2 hours before serving.

PEAR-CRANBERRY UPSIDE-DOWN CAKE

MAKES 1 CAKE, ENOUGH TO SERVE 8 TO 10

A DESSERT AS SEASONAL AS this warms the home as well as the senses with its fruity sweetness and homey appeal. An added attraction is that this cake reheats beautifully, making it a prime candidate for make-ahead baking.

½ pound (2 sticks) unsalted butter

1¼ cups light brown sugar

1 cup sweetened dried cranberries or dried cherries

4 ripe pears, peeled, cored, halved and sliced into ¼-inch slices and held in 1 tablespoon lemon juice plus ½ cup water

1 cup granulated sugar

2 eggs

2 cups sifted cake flour

2 teaspoons baking powder

Fine sea salt

1 teaspoon vanilla extract

¾ cup milk

1. Preheat the oven to 350°F.

2. Cook 1 stick of the butter and the brown sugar together in a small saucepan, stirring, over low heat, until the butter and sugar melt and dissolve into a syrup.

3. Arrange the pear slices in an overlapping circular pattern on the bottom of a 9-inch nonstick, round cake pan. Sprinkle the dried cranberries over the pears. Pour the butter-sugar syrup over the pears and cranberries.

4. Cream the remaining stick of butter and the granulated sugar together in the bowl of an electric mixer, scraping down the sides of the bowl occasionally, then add the eggs, one at a time, combine well, and scrape down again. In a bowl combine the sifted flour, baking powder, and ½ teaspoon salt. Add the flour mixture slowly to the egg mixture while beating continuously. Add the vanilla and milk and beat just until combined.

MAKE THIS CAKE WITH APPLES instead of pears, or currants in place of cranberries.

5. Pour the batter over the fruit at the bottom of the cake pan. Bake until a skewer inserted into the cake comes out clean, about 25 minutes. Let the cake rest in the pan on a rack to cool.

6. To serve, slide a knife around the edge of the pan and carefully unmold the cake onto a serving platter.

TOASTED COCONUT MERINGUE AND WARM WINTER FRUITS

MAKES 10 TO 12 MERINGUE SHELLS

WALK THROUGH most European pastry shops and you'll notice baked meringue, all white and crisp and light. Not only light in weight, but in the mouth. In addition to its appealing texture, toasted meringue delivers a very satisfying sugar shot. Fill it with fruits and it's the perfect make-ahead dessert for the holidays.

1 cup egg whites (about 8 separated eggs; reserve the yolks for another use like flan or custard)

1 teaspoon freshly squeezed lemon juice

1½ cups superfine sugar

1 cup shredded coconut (preferably unsweetened)

4 tablespoons (½ stick) unsalted butter

2 pears, peeled and cut into ½-inch dice

2 apples, peeled and cut into ½-inch dice

½ cup diced dried figs

½ cup diced dried apricots

¼ cup raisins

1 teaspoon ground cinnamon

¼ cup maple syrup

½ cup granulated sugar

¼ cup orange liqueur

½ cup sliced blanched almonds

1. Preheat the oven to 200°F.

2. Put the egg whites and lemon juice in the bowl of a standing mixer fitted with the whip attachment. Whip the whites to soft peaks. Add 1 cup of the superfine sugar while continuing to whip. Continue to whip to stiff but not dry peaks while adding the remaining ½ cup superfine sugar. Using a spatula, gently fold in the coconut, being careful not to deflate the whites.

3. Put the mixture in a pastry bag fitted with the star tip. Line a cookie sheet with parchment paper. For each shell, pipe out a 3-inch ring, then top with another ring to achieve height. Continue in this manner until you have used all of the mixture; you should have 10 to 12 meringue shells.

VARY THE PROPORTION OF
FRUIT, or use only one type to
focus on its flavor.

Bake until the meringues are dry, about 1 hour. Turn off the oven and leave the meringues in the oven to continue to dry for 6 hours or overnight. The meringues can be kept in a cool, dry place for up to 1 week.

4. Put the butter in a sauté pan and set the pan over medium heat. Add the pears and apples and sauté just until the fruit begins to caramelize, about 8 minutes. Add the figs, apricots, raisins, and cinnamon. Add the maple syrup, granulated sugar, liqueur, and ¼ cup water and cook for 10 minutes to stew the dried fruit. Remove the pan from the heat and let cool slightly.

5. Spoon the fruit into the meringue shells, top with sliced almonds, and serve.

SILKY COCONUT FLAN

SERVES 6

Fʟᴀɴ, ᴏʀ ᴄʀᴇ̀ᴍᴇ ᴄᴀʀᴀᴍᴇʟ, is easy to pull off with style: you make a caramel syrup, coat custard cups with it, pour in a custard, and refrigerate. When ready to serve, you simply invert the cup onto a plate; the custard pops out with the caramel running down its sides in dramatic fashion. Flan can be made a day or two in advance and served on demand.

1½ cups sugar

1½ cups milk

½ cup heavy cream

1 cup unsweetened coconut milk

1 cinnamon stick

6 eggs

4 egg yolks

½ cup toasted coconut

2 tablespoons grated lemon zest

1. Preheat the oven to 325°F.

2. In a pot, combine 1 cup of the sugar and ¼ cup water and cook over low heat until the sugar melts. Continue to cook until the sugar has caramelized to a rich golden brown. Carefully pour the caramel into six 4-ounce ramekins or heatproof crème caramel, flan, or pudding cups, turning the cups to coat the bottom and sides with an even layer. Set aside to let the caramel cool and harden.

3. Combine the milk, the remaining ½ cup sugar, cream, coconut milk, and cinnamon stick in a saucepan and set over low heat. Bring to a simmer and continue to simmer gently for 30 minutes. Use tongs or a slotted spoon to remove and discard the cinnamon stick, then set the pan aside and let the mixture cool for 15 minutes.

4. Break the eggs into a bowl, add the yolks, beat with a whisk, and gradually beat the hot milk mixture into the eggs in a thin, slow stream, a little

GARNISH THE FLAN WITH
FRESH FRUITS such as diced
oranges and pineapple, fresh
blackberries, mango, or papaya.
For a "regular" flan, replace the
coconut milk with whole milk,
omit the cinnamon, and add
½ teaspoon vanilla extract to
the pot along with the milk.

at a time to avoid cooking the eggs. Pour the coconut mixture through a
fine-mesh strainer into a large, heatproof measuring cup to facilitate pouring it into the custard cups.

5.   Put the flan dishes in a baking pan. Put the baking pan on the middle
rack of the oven and fill the flan dishes with the coconut mixture. Pour
warm water into the baking pan to create a water bath coming halfway up
the sides of the cups. Bake until the custards are completely set and a
toothpick inserted to the center of a flan comes out clean, 20 to 25 minutes. Remove from the oven, use tongs to carefully remove the cups from
the water bath, and let cool completely. Cover each cup with plastic wrap
and refrigerate for at least 6 hours, or overnight. Keep refrigerated until
ready to serve.

6.   To serve, run a sharp knife around the inside of the flan dish to loosen. Invert the dish onto a plate and pop out the flan. The caramel should pour
down the sides of the custard. Garnish with toasted coconut and lemon zest.

POACHED PEARS AND MASCARPONE WITH ESPRESSO SAUCE

MAKES 4 LARGE PORTIONS OR 6 TO 8 SMALL PORTIONS

POACHED PEARS ARE AN END IN THEMSELVES, *a fall treat to be enjoyed with vanilla ice cream or a soothing cup of tea. So, when you dress up poached pears with not one but two irresistible flourishes—in this case mascarpone and rich espresso sauce—you're going the extra mile and treating yourself and your guests to something special.*

½ cup dry white wine

¼ cup sugar

1 cinnamon stick

3 whole cloves

½ cup good-quality port wine

4 firm Bartlett pears

1 cup Italian mascarpone or other fresh sweet cow's-milk cheese

¼ cup milk

2 tablespoons clover honey

¼ teaspoon vanilla extract

½ teaspoon ground cinnamon

¼ teaspoon ground nutmeg

Espresso Sauce (recipe follows)

2 tablespoons poppy seeds

2 tablespoons dried cherries

1. Put the wine, sugar, cinnamon stick, cloves, port, and 3 cups water in a heavy-bottomed pot just large enough to hold the pears. Bring to a boil over high heat, then lower the heat and simmer for 5 minutes. While the poaching liquid is cooking, peel but do not core the pears; use a vegetable peeler for the neatest job with the least waste.

2. Add the pears to the simmering liquid and poach them until they are just tender to the tip of a knife, about 20 minutes. Remove from the heat and cool the pears in the liquid for another 20 minutes, then cover and refrigerate.

3. In a stainless-steel bowl, combine the mascarpone, milk, honey, vanilla, cinnamon, and nutmeg and whisk to form a smooth, creamy filling. Put the filling into a clean pastry bag fitted with a star tip.

INSTEAD OF POACHED PEARS, serve the espresso sauce over fresh strawberries, raspberries, vanilla ice cream, or—if you love coffee—coffee ice cream.

IF YOU CAN'T FIND MASCAR-PONE, use whipped cream cheese in its place.

4. Remove the pears from the liquid and drain and dry them. Cut the pears in half lengthwise and remove the core with a teaspoon, making a neat opening to be filled with the mascarpone filling. Slice a sliver off the bottom or outside of the pear to steady it on the plate.

5. Pipe a neat star-shaped dollop of filling into the pear, pour some espresso sauce around, and garnish with poppy seeds and dried cherries.

ESPRESSO SAUCE

1 cup milk	4 egg yolks
½ cup heavy cream	⅓ cup sugar
1 vanilla bean	¼ cup strong espresso coffee

1. Pour the milk and heavy cream into a heavy-bottomed pot. On a cutting board, split the vanilla bean down the middle and, using the tip of your knife, scrape all the seeds into the milk. Add the bean pod to the milk and bring the milk gently to a boil over medium heat, being careful not to scorch the milk or allow it to boil over. Lower the heat and simmer for 10 minutes, uncovered. Remove from the heat and allow the vanilla bean to steep in the milk for another 5 minutes.

2. Meanwhile, in the bowl of an electric mixer, whip the egg yolks and sugar together at medium speed for 5 minutes. Remove the vanilla bean from the milk, then stir several tablespoons of the hot milk into the egg yolk–sugar mixture to temper the eggs.

3. Fill a large bowl halfway with ice water. Return the pot of milk to the stove and, over low heat, add the egg yolk–sugar mixture in a slow, steady stream, stirring it in with a wooden spoon. Stir the coffee into the sauce with a wooden spoon and continue to cook for 7 to 8 minutes, stirring constantly, until the custard has thickened and coats the back of the spoon. Remove from the heat and cool completely by setting the bottom of the pot in the ice water and stirring to release the heat. Once cool, the sauce can be covered and refrigerated for up to 24 hours.

PLUM AND PEACH COBBLER

SERVES 6 TO 8

COBBLERS ARE JUST THE THING TO MAKE *when fresh fruit is plentiful. I like cobblers with any seasonal fruit except melons. The best fruit for cobblers are berries and stone fruit such as peaches, plums, and cherries. Long the staple of true country cooking, they are a very forgiving dessert. Be creative. Serve warm with ice cream or whipped cream.*

1 pound ripe black plums or other plums, cut into eighths

1 pound fresh, ripe peaches, halved

1 cup plus 3 tablespoons sugar, plus more for sprinkling

1½ teaspoons ground cinnamon

1 tablespoon cornstarch

¼ cup orange liqueur such as Grand Marnier

1½ cups sifted all-purpose flour, plus more for dusting a work surface

1 teaspoon baking powder

Fine sea salt

¾ cup buttermilk

8 tablespoons (1 stick) cold unsalted butter, cut into small pieces, plus melted butter for brushing

1. Preheat the oven to 375°F.

2. Stir the fruit together in a bowl with the 1 cup sugar, the cinnamon, cornstarch, and orange liqueur. Pour into a 3- to 4-quart casserole or soufflé dish.

3. Stir the flour, remaining 3 tablespoons sugar, baking powder, and ¼ teaspoon salt together in a bowl until thoroughly mixed. Add the buttermilk to the bowl and combine. Add the cold butter quickly, combining only briefly with a fork, to leave the mixture as lumpy as possible, which helps make a flaky crust.

NIGHTLY SPECIALS

FEEL FREE TO USE STRAWBER-RIES and/or blueberries in place of the plums and peaches. Or use peeled, diced apples and increase the cooking time to approximately 35 minutes.

4. Lightly flour a work surface and dump the lumpy pastry out onto it. Flatten gently with your hands or a rolling pin into a shape about 1 inch thick. Cut the pastry into 2-inch circles or squares, using all the pastry. Top the fruit with the pastry, brush with melted butter, sprinkle the top with sugar, and bake until the pastry top is nicely browned, 20 to 25 minutes. Serve warm.

BAKED ALASKA WITH COCONUT SORBET AND CHOCOLATE ICE CREAM

SERVES 8 TO 10

BAKED ALASKA HAS BEEN FLOATING AROUND as a dessert since Thomas Jefferson's day, albeit with different names. Fannie Farmer is said to have named this masterwork of confection—ice cream and sorbet surrounded by toasted meringue. The ice cream and sorbet bombe can be kept frozen for weeks before being covered with meringue and toasted. You can use a store-bought sponge cake and skip steps 1 through 5. You can also, of course, make this with store-bought ice cream and sorbet. In any case, you will need a 2-quart ice cream bombe mold.

BAKED ALASKA

3 egg yolks

6 tablespoons plus ¼ cup sugar

1 teaspoon vanilla extract

8 egg whites (in 2 bowls of 4 whites each)

1½ cups all-purpose flour, sifted

Coconut Sorbet (recipe follows)

Chocolate Ice Cream (recipe follows)

1. Preheat the oven to 425°F.

2. First make the sponge cake: In a bowl, whip the egg yolks with 2 tablespoons of the sugar and the vanilla until creamy and yellow.

3. In another bowl, whip 4 of the egg whites to soft peaks, add the remaining 4 tablespoons sugar, and continue to whip the whites to stiff peaks.

4. Carefully fold the beaten egg whites into the yolk-sugar mixture. Using the same care, fold in the sifted flour.

5. Line a cookie sheet with parchment paper, pour the cake batter onto the sheet, and spread out the batter to evenly coat the sheet. Bake on the oven's center rack until the top is golden brown, 12 to 15 minutes. Remove from the oven and cool the cake quickly on a rack near an open window.

6. Begin to assemble the baked Alaska by cutting the sponge cake in 2 pieces to the shape of the bombe mold. (Cut a large piece for lining the mold and a smaller piece for the top, which later will be inverted to become the bottom.)

7. Line the bombe mold with plastic wrap and then place the larger piece of cake on top of the plastic.

8. Remove the sorbet and ice cream from the freezer and allow to soften for 10 minutes. Spoon or scoop the sorbet into the cake-lined mold, creating an even layer. Cover the sorbet with the ice cream in the same fashion, smoothing out the ice cream into one even layer. Place the remaining layer of cake on top of the ice cream layer to act as a seal. Freeze the bombe for 4 to 5 hours, or up to 2 weeks.

9. Preheat the oven to 450°F.

10. To finish the Alaska, whip the remaining 4 egg whites to soft peaks, add the ¼ cup sugar, and continue to whip to stiff but not dry peaks. (This is your meringue.) Pour the meringue into a pastry bag fitted with a star tip. Unmold the bombe. Use hot towels to help loosen the bombe if necessary and invert the bombe onto a heatproof serving platter.

11. Remove the plastic wrap and pipe a decorative design of meringue all around the base of the bombe. Cover the entire bombe with this meringue in as decorative a design as you can manage, being as creative as you like, but working quickly to avoid melting too much of the ice cream and sorbet. Bake the Alaska for just 5 minutes, to lightly brown the meringue but not melt the ice cream.

12. Remove the baked Alaska from the oven, slice into individual servings, and serve immediately.

COCONUT SORBET
MAKES 3 CUPS SORBET

8 ounces sweetened coconut milk   ½ cup toasted coconut

1. Combine the coconut milk and 2 cups water and chill for several hours in the refrigerator.

2. Freeze the mixture in an ice cream freezer according to the manufacturer's instructions. Stir the toasted coconut into the frozen coconut sorbet. Keep frozen till ready to serve.

USE DIFFERENT FLAVORS OF
ICE CREAM AND SORBET.
Purchase if you prefer not to
make them.

CHOCOLATE ICE CREAM
MAKES 5 CUPS ICE CREAM

4 ounces semisweet chocolate	2 cups milk
3 egg yolks	2 cups heavy cream
½ cup sugar	1 vanilla bean, split

1. Melt the chocolate in the top of a double boiler, stirring occasionally, and being careful not to scorch the bottom.

2. Combine the egg yolks and the sugar in a bowl and whip to a creamy and smooth yellow.

3. Combine the milk, cream, and vanilla bean in a pot over medium heat and bring to a boil. Lower the heat and let simmer.

4. Whisk one-third of the hot milk mixture into the egg-sugar mixture to temper the eggs. Stir. Pour the tempered mixture into the remaining hot milk mixture while whisking the milk with a wire whisk. Stir with a wooden spoon until the hot milk-egg mixture thickens enough to coat the back of the spoon.

5. Add the melted chocolate to the hot milk-egg mixture by whipping it in with a wire whisk.

6. Strain the mixture through a fine-mesh strainer and cool quickly in an ice bath. Refrigerate the mixture for several hours before freezing.

7. Freeze the mixture in an ice cream freezer according to the manufacturer's directions. Keep frozen till ready to serve.

FLOURLESS CHOCOLATE CAKE

SERVES 10 TO 12

A TRUE MODERN CLASSIC, *the flourless chocolate cake is no longer a novelty. But it is satisfying enough to have stood the test of time and remain relevant as a dessert in its own right, regardless of its dietary appeal.*

½ cup granulated sugar

¾ cup light corn syrup

10 ounces good-quality semisweet chocolate, preferably French or Belgian, coarsely chopped

8 tablespoons (1 stick) unsalted butter, at room temperature, plus more for greasing the pan

3 eggs

2 egg yolks

Confectioners' sugar, for dusting

1.   Bring the granulated sugar and corn syrup to a boil in a heavy-bottomed pot over high heat. Reduce the heat to low and simmer for 5 minutes. Remove from the heat and let cool slightly, 5 minutes.

2.   Melt the chocolate in the top of a double boiler over simmering water, stirring the chocolate occasionally. Remove the pot from the heat and whisk in the butter until well incorporated. Avoid getting any liquid, like water or condensation from the double boiler, into the pot because it will cause the chocolate to seize up into a solid mass. Set aside the chocolate to let it cool slightly, 5 minutes.

3.   With an electric mixer, beat the eggs and yolks at medium-high speed until frothy, 5 to 6 minutes. Lower the speed to a medium-low setting and carefully pour the still-hot sugar syrup into the beaten eggs. Remove the bowl from the machine, and using a rubber spatula fold the chocolate into the egg mixture, then stir with the spatula to a smooth consistency.

4.   Preheat the oven to 350°F.

TOP WITH YOUR FAVORITE
FRUITS (cherries would be delicious) or serve with a scoop of ice
cream. Vanilla would be delicious;
so would pistachio, coffee, or
amaretto.

5. Lightly butter a 9-inch round springform cake pan with a removable bottom and pour in the chocolate mixture. Put the cake pan on a cookie sheet to catch any spillage. Bake until the top of the cake has risen and set, 45 to 50 minutes.

6. Remove the cookie sheet from the oven, and set the cake pan on a cooling rack.

7. Cool the cake completely to room temperature before unmolding. Run a sharp knife around the inner circumference of the pan. Unclasp the hinge and, if necessary, tap the bottom of the pan with a knife, or run a knife under the bottom of the cake, to help release the cake. Let cool at room temperature for at least 2 hours, or refrigerate overnight. Bring to room temperature before serving.

8. Top with a light dusting of confectioners' sugar and slice into individual servings.

FROZEN GRAND MARNIER SOUFFLÉ

SERVES 4

OKAY, THESE AREN'T ACTUALLY SOUFFLÉS, but they appear to be: risen precariously and seemingly ready to fall at any second. In reality, they are filled with orange mousse, light, frothy, and softly frozen. This recipe falls into one of my favorite categories, the Mandatory Make-Ahead Dessert. Because it has to be chilled before it's served, it doesn't give you any choice other than to get its preparation out of the way early.

8 whole eggs

1 cup granulated sugar, plus more for coating the ramekins

Unsalted butter, softened for greasing the ramekins

1½ cups heavy cream

3 tablespoons confectioners' sugar

¼ cup Grand Marnier

3 tablespoons orange zest

Whipped cream, for serving

1 orange, segmented

1. Combine the eggs and granulated sugar in the pot of a double boiler set over simmering water, whisking constantly and being careful not to scramble the eggs. Continue to whisk over low heat until the mixture is golden in color and thick enough to coat the back of a spoon and fall in ribbons as you lift the spoon from the pot. Remove from the heat and set the mixture aside to cool.

2. Meanwhile, prepare four 1-cup soufflé dishes or ramekins: Butter the inside of the dish, then sprinkle with granulated sugar, tapping out any excess sugar onto a plate. Cut pieces of waxed paper long enough to wrap each soufflé dish twice around its circumference like a collar and stand 3 to 4 inches above its rim. Wrap the waxed paper snugly around the outside of the dish and seal the edges with transparent tape, snugly fitting the waxed paper to the dish.

POSSIBLE SUBSTITUTIONS FOR
THE GRAND MARNIER: almond
liqueur, hazelnut liqueur (like
Frangelico), or chocolate liqueur
(like Godiva)—same quantities
for all.

3. Using an electric mixer, combine 1 cup of the heavy cream, 2 table-spoons of the confectioners' sugar, the Grand Marnier, and orange zest and whip until firm peaks form. With a spatula, gently fold the whipped cream mixture into the cooled egg mixture. Divide the mixture among the buttered soufflé dishes, filling them above the rim and in contact with the waxed paper, which will hold the moisture in.

4. Put the soufflés in the freezer for at least 4 hours, or preferably overnight. When they are fully frozen and firm to a knife-tip, carefully remove the waxed paper collar.

5. Whip the remaining ½ cup cream with the remaining 1 tablespoon confectioners' sugar. To serve, top each serving with a dollop of whipped cream and orange segments.

CHOCOLATE TRUFFLES

MAKES 70 TO 75 TRUFFLES

TRUFFLES ARE A UNIVERSAL FAVORITE, rich, elegant, and satisfying. So what makes them a nightly special? Well, to my mind, they're one of those things that are savored only on rare occasions. I recommend them to you as a great holiday gift, or personal indulgence at the conclusion of an ambitious home-cooked meal. Truffles are easier to make than you may think. You might especially like to make them with children, who enjoy the process more than anyone. In fact, my goddaughter joined me on my program Michael's Place to help me demonstrate this recipe. (Be sure to carefully supervise kids if you do this with them.)

2 pounds high-quality semisweet chocolate, preferably Belgian or French

½ cup heavy cream

8 tablespoons (1 stick) unsalted butter, softened and cut into chunks

1 teaspoon vanilla extract

1. Melt 1 pound of the chocolate, slowly stirring, in a double boiler set over simmering water.

2. Warm the cream in a large saucepan over medium heat, being careful not to scorch it.

3. Remove the chocolate from the heat, let cool slightly, then stir into the heavy cream. Remove the chocolate-cream mixture from the heat and let cool for 5 minutes.

4. Stir the butter and vanilla into the chocolate-cream mixture. Transfer to a heatproof bowl, cover with plastic wrap, and chill in the refrigerator until firm but still pliable, about 20 minutes.

5. Transfer the chocolate mixture to a pastry bag fitted with a #5 tip and pipe teaspoon-size mounds on a waxed paper–covered cookie sheet, or

AFTER FORMING CHOCOLATE BALLS IN STEP 6, REFRIGERATE. Once chilled, truffles can be rolled in shredded coconut, crushed nuts, cocoa powder, or other coatings. If rolled in coconut or nuts, they can then be dipped in chocolate, as in step 7.

FOR A DIFFERENT RENDERING OF THE SAME FLAVORS, dip the truffles in chocolate in step 7, then, while they are still wet, dip them in shredded coconut, chopped nuts, or other coatings.

YOU CAN ALSO ADD 2 TABLESPOONS ORANGE LIQUEUR along with the vanilla in step 4 to infuse the truffles with an elegant scent.

use a spoon to dole out teaspoon-size mounds. Refrigerate the entire sheet until the chocolate mixture is hard to the touch, about 30 minutes. (The recipe can be made to this point, or up to the end of step 6, up to 2 days in advance.)

6.   When the chocolate mixture is sufficiently firm, remove from the refrigerator and, working quickly to prevent melting, roll the chocolate mounds into balls, then chill the balls again until firm on a waxed paper–covered sheet. (The recipe can be made to this point up to 2 days in advance. Be sure to cover the balls with waxed paper if refrigerating for more than a few hours.)

7.   Melt the remaining 1 pound chocolate in a double boiler set over simmering water. Remove the double boiler from the heat and let cool slightly. Using a wire dipping spoon or a regular teaspoon, with your hands in latex gloves, make the truffles by dipping each ball briefly into the melted chocolate. Place on a cake rack set over a cookie sheet until dry and refrigerate until firm. You may scrape up any chocolate that has dripped on the cookie sheet and return it to the dipping pot for more dipping. The truffles will keep for several weeks if refrigerated in an airtight container.

cornmeal (*Continued*)

    in savory chipotle chile muffins, 246

    soft herbed polenta, 113

couscous:

    for Moroccan lamb stew, 82–83

    Sicilian shrimp and, 130–31

    vegetarian, 131

crab(s):

    cakes, Maryland-style, 117–19

    grilled soft-shell, with lime, rum, and mango, 120–21

    soft-shell, sandwich with chile mayonnaise, 121

cranberry:

    -pear upside-down cake, 270–71

    relish, uncooked, 182

cream, heavy:

    in chicken pot pie, 76–78

    in chocolate ice cream, 285

    in creamed spinach with bacon, 252–53

    in fettuccine with mushrooms and asparagus, 87–88

    in frozen Grand Marnier soufflé, 288–89

    in mashed potatoes, 236–37

    in potato gratin, 234–35

    in roasted corn chowder with shrimp and tarragon, 70–72

    in roasted oysters with country bacon, 122–23

    in silky coconut flan, 274–76

crème fraîche, 64

in curried pea soup with frizzled ginger, 63–66

in leek and onion tartlets with American caviar, 37–39

croutons, 16

Cuban sandwiches, 221

Cuban-style black bean soup, 73–75

cucumber:

    in charred beef and crisp vegetables, 26–27

    in tamarind-glazed shrimp salad, 29–30

curly endive salad with warm bacon vinaigrette, 15–16

currants, dried, quinoa "risotto" with toasted hazelnuts and, 106–7

curried:

    pea soup with frizzled ginger, 63–66

    wheat berries with sweet onions, 108–9

frozen Grand Marnier soufflé, 288–89

pear-cranberry upside-down cake, 270–71

pie dough, basic, 266–67

plum and peach cobbler, 280–81

poached pears and mascarpone with espresso sauce, 277–79

silky coconut flan, 274–76

toasted coconut meringue and warm winter fruits, 272–73

triple berry and pecan crunch pie, 268–69

dill, marinated salmon carpaccio with green apple and, 31–32

double-crust apple pie, 264–65

duck:

    breast, black currant–lacquered, 193–94

    roasted Long Island, with rhubarb compote, 196–97

D

desserts, 263–92

    baked Alaska with coconut sorbet and chocolate ice cream, 282–85

    chocolate truffles, 291–92

    double-crust apple pie, 264–65

    flourless chocolate cake, 286–87

E

eggplant:

    boneless roast leg of lamb with feta, olives and, 228–29

    in grilled vegetable and Jack cheese sandwich, 46–47